metrix

TEST PREPARATION

crets of the onderlic® ersonnel Test- uicktest tudy Guide

DEAR FUTURE EXAM SUCCESS STORY

First of all, **THANK YOU** for purchasing Mometrix study materials!

Second, congratulations! You are one of the few determined test-takers who are committed to doing whatever it takes to excel on your exam. **You have come to the right place.** We developed these study materials with one goal in mind: to deliver you the information you need in a format that's concise and easy to use.

In addition to optimizing your guide for the content of the test, we've outlined our recommended steps for breaking down the preparation process into small, attainable goals so you can make sure you stay on track.

We've also analyzed the entire test-taking process, identifying the most common pitfalls and showing how you can overcome them and be ready for any curveball the test throws you.

Standardized testing is one of the biggest obstacles on your road to success, which only increases the importance of doing well in the high-pressure, high-stakes environment of test day. Your results on this test could have a significant impact on your future, and this guide provides the information and practical advice to help you achieve your full potential on test day.

Your success is our success

We would love to hear from you! If you would like to share the story of your exam success or if you have any questions or comments in regard to our products, please contact us at **800-673-8175** or **support@mometrix.com**.

Thanks again for your business and we wish you continued success!

Sincerely,
The Mometrix Test Preparation Team

Need more help? Check out our flashcards at:
http://MometrixFlashcards.com/Wonderlic

Written and edited by the Mometrix Exam Secrets Test Prep Team
Printed in the United States of America

TABLE OF CONTENTS

INTRODUCTION 1
SECRET KEY #1 – PLAN BIG, STUDY SMALL 2
SECRET KEY #2 – MAKE YOUR STUDYING COUNT 3
SECRET KEY #3 – PRACTICE THE RIGHT WAY 4
SECRET KEY #4 – PACE YOURSELF 6
SECRET KEY #5 – HAVE A PLAN FOR GUESSING 7
TEST-TAKING STRATEGIES 10
VERBAL REVIEW 15
FINAL NOTES 17
MATHEMATICS REVIEW 18
NUMBERS AND THEIR CLASSIFICATIONS 18
OPERATIONS 19
POSITIVE AND NEGATIVE NUMBERS 22
FACTORS AND MULTIPLES 23
FRACTIONS, PERCENTAGES, AND RELATED CONCEPTS 23
SYSTEMS OF EQUATIONS 26
POLYNOMIAL ALGEBRA 28
SPECIAL REPORT: WONDERLIC SECRETS IN ACTION 29
SAMPLE MATH QUESTION: 29
PRACTICE TEST #1 31
ANSWER KEY AND EXPLANATIONS FOR TEST #1 37
PRACTICE TEST #2 40
ANSWER KEY AND EXPLANATIONS FOR TEST #2 45
PRACTICE TEST #3 48
ANSWER KEY AND EXPLANATIONS FOR TEST #3 54
WONDERLIC SKILL BUILDING QUESTIONS 57
MATHEMATICS PRACTICE 1 57
ANSWER KEY FOR MATHEMATICS PRACTICE 1 64
VERBAL PRACTICE 1 66
ANSWER KEY FOR VERBAL PRACTICE 1 70
MATHEMATICS PRACTICE 2 71
ANSWER KEY FOR MATHEMATICS PRACTICE 2 78
VERBAL PRACTICE 2 80
ANSWER KEY FOR VERBAL PRACTICE 2 84
HOW TO OVERCOME TEST ANXIETY 85

ONLINE RESOURCES 91

Introduction

Thank you for purchasing this resource! You have made the choice to prepare yourself for a test that could have a huge impact on your future, and this guide is designed to help you be fully ready for test day. Obviously, it's important to have a solid understanding of the test material, but you also need to be prepared for the unique environment and stressors of the test, so that you can perform to the best of your abilities.

For this purpose, the first section that appears in this guide is the **Secret Keys**. We've devoted countless hours to meticulously researching what works and what doesn't, and we've boiled down our findings to the five most impactful steps you can take to improve your performance on the test. We start at the beginning with study planning and move through the preparation process, all the way to the testing strategies that will help you get the most out of what you know when you're finally sitting in front of the test.

We recommend that you start preparing for your test as far in advance as possible. However, if you've bought this guide as a last-minute study resource and only have a few days before your test, we recommend that you skip over the first two Secret Keys since they address a long-term study plan.

If you struggle with **test anxiety**, we strongly encourage you to check out our recommendations for how you can overcome it. Test anxiety is a formidable foe, but it can be beaten, and we want to make sure you have the tools you need to defeat it.

Secret Key #1 – Plan Big, Study Small

There's a lot riding on your performance. If you want to ace this test, you're going to need to keep your skills sharp and the material fresh in your mind. You need a plan that lets you review everything you need to know while still fitting in your schedule. We'll break this strategy down into three categories.

Information Organization

Start with the information you already have: the official test outline. From this, you can make a complete list of all the concepts you need to cover before the test. Organize these concepts into groups that can be studied together, and create a list of any related vocabulary you need to learn so you can brush up on any difficult terms. You'll want to keep this vocabulary list handy once you actually start studying since you may need to add to it along the way.

Time Management

Once you have your set of study concepts, decide how to spread them out over the time you have left before the test. Break your study plan into small, clear goals so you have a manageable task for each day and know exactly what you're doing. Then just focus on one small step at a time. When you manage your time this way, you don't need to spend hours at a time studying. Studying a small block of content for a short period each day helps you retain information better and avoid stressing over how much you have left to do. You can relax knowing that you have a plan to cover everything in time. In order for this strategy to be effective though, you have to start studying early and stick to your schedule. Avoid the exhaustion and futility that comes from last-minute cramming!

Study Environment

The environment you study in has a big impact on your learning. Studying in a coffee shop, while probably more enjoyable, is not likely to be as fruitful as studying in a quiet room. It's important to keep distractions to a minimum. You're only planning to study for a short block of time, so make the most of it. Don't pause to check your phone or get up to find a snack. It's also important to **avoid multitasking**. Research has consistently shown that multitasking will make your studying dramatically less effective. Your study area should also be comfortable and well-lit so you don't have the distraction of straining your eyes or sitting on an uncomfortable chair.

The time of day you study is also important. You want to be rested and alert. Don't wait until just before bedtime. Study when you'll be most likely to comprehend and remember. Even better, if you know what time of day your test will be, set that time aside for study. That way your brain will be used to working on that subject at that specific time and you'll have a better chance of recalling information.

Finally, it can be helpful to team up with others who are studying for the same test. Your actual studying should be done in as isolated an environment as possible, but the work of organizing the information and setting up the study plan can be divided up. In between study sessions, you can discuss with your teammates the concepts that you're all studying and quiz each other on the details. Just be sure that your teammates are as serious about the test as you are. If you find that your study time is being replaced with social time, you might need to find a new team.

Secret Key #2 – Make Your Studying Count

You're devoting a lot of time and effort to preparing for this test, so you want to be absolutely certain it will pay off. This means doing more than just reading the content and hoping you can remember it on test day. It's important to make every minute of study count. There are two main areas you can focus on to make your studying count.

Retention

It doesn't matter how much time you study if you can't remember the material. You need to make sure you are retaining the concepts. To check your retention of the information you're learning, try recalling it at later times with minimal prompting. Try carrying around flashcards and glance at one or two from time to time or ask a friend who's also studying for the test to quiz you.

To enhance your retention, look for ways to put the information into practice so that you can apply it rather than simply recalling it. If you're using the information in practical ways, it will be much easier to remember. Similarly, it helps to solidify a concept in your mind if you're not only reading it to yourself but also explaining it to someone else. Ask a friend to let you teach them about a concept you're a little shaky on (or speak aloud to an imaginary audience if necessary). As you try to summarize, define, give examples, and answer your friend's questions, you'll understand the concepts better and they will stay with you longer. Finally, step back for a big picture view and ask yourself how each piece of information fits with the whole subject. When you link the different concepts together and see them working together as a whole, it's easier to remember the individual components.

Finally, practice showing your work on any multi-step problems, even if you're just studying. Writing out each step you take to solve a problem will help solidify the process in your mind, and you'll be more likely to remember it during the test.

Modality

Modality simply refers to the means or method by which you study. Choosing a study modality that fits your own individual learning style is crucial. No two people learn best in exactly the same way, so it's important to know your strengths and use them to your advantage.

For example, if you learn best by visualization, focus on visualizing a concept in your mind and draw an image or a diagram. Try color-coding your notes, illustrating them, or creating symbols that will trigger your mind to recall a learned concept. If you learn best by hearing or discussing information, find a study partner who learns the same way or read aloud to yourself. Think about how to put the information in your own words. Imagine that you are giving a lecture on the topic and record yourself so you can listen to it later.

For any learning style, flashcards can be helpful. Organize the information so you can take advantage of spare moments to review. Underline key words or phrases. Use different colors for different categories. Mnemonic devices (such as creating a short list in which every item starts with the same letter) can also help with retention. Find what works best for you and use it to store the information in your mind most effectively and easily.

Secret Key #3 – Practice the Right Way

Your success on test day depends not only on how many hours you put into preparing, but also on whether you prepared the right way. It's good to check along the way to see if your studying is paying off. One of the most effective ways to do this is by taking practice tests to evaluate your progress. Practice tests are useful because they show exactly where you need to improve. Every time you take a practice test, pay special attention to these three groups of questions:

- The questions you got wrong
- The questions you had to guess on, even if you guessed right
- The questions you found difficult or slow to work through

This will show you exactly what your weak areas are, and where you need to devote more study time. Ask yourself why each of these questions gave you trouble. Was it because you didn't understand the material? Was it because you didn't remember the vocabulary? Do you need more repetitions on this type of question to build speed and confidence? Dig into those questions and figure out how you can strengthen your weak areas as you go back to review the material.

Additionally, many practice tests have a section explaining the answer choices. It can be tempting to read the explanation and think that you now have a good understanding of the concept. However, an explanation likely only covers part of the question's broader context. Even if the explanation makes perfect sense, **go back and investigate** every concept related to the question until you're positive you have a thorough understanding.

As you go along, keep in mind that the practice test is just that: practice. Memorizing these questions and answers will not be very helpful on the actual test because it is unlikely to have any of the same exact questions. If you only know the right answers to the sample questions, you won't be prepared for the real thing. **Study the concepts** until you understand them fully, and then you'll be able to answer any question that shows up on the test.

It's important to wait on the practice tests until you're ready. If you take a test on your first day of study, you may be overwhelmed by the amount of material covered and how much you need to learn. Work up to it gradually.

On test day, you'll need to be prepared for answering questions, managing your time, and using the test-taking strategies you've learned. It's a lot to balance, like a mental marathon that will have a big impact on your future. Like training for a marathon, you'll need to start slowly and work your way up. When test day arrives, you'll be ready.

Start with the strategies you've read in the first two Secret Keys—plan your course and study in the way that works best for you. If you have time, consider using multiple study resources to get different approaches to the same concepts. It can be helpful to see difficult concepts from more than one angle. Then find a good source for practice tests. Many times, the test website will suggest potential study resources or provide sample tests.

Practice Test Strategy

If you're able to find at least three practice tests, we recommend this strategy:

Untimed and Open-Book Practice

Take the first test with no time constraints and with your notes and study guide handy. Take your time and focus on applying the strategies you've learned.

Timed and Open-Book Practice

Take the second practice test open-book as well, but set a timer and practice pacing yourself to finish in time.

Timed and Closed-Book Practice

Take any other practice tests as if it were test day. Set a timer and put away your study materials. Sit at a table or desk in a quiet room, imagine yourself at the testing center, and answer questions as quickly and accurately as possible.

Keep repeating timed and closed-book tests on a regular basis until you run out of practice tests or it's time for the actual test. Your mind will be ready for the schedule and stress of test day, and you'll be able to focus on recalling the material you've learned.

Secret Key #4 – Pace Yourself

Once you're fully prepared for the material on the test, your biggest challenge on test day will be managing your time. Just knowing that the clock is ticking can make you panic even if you have plenty of time left. Work on pacing yourself so you can build confidence against the time constraints of the exam. Pacing is a difficult skill to master, especially in a high-pressure environment, so **practice is vital**.

Set time expectations for your pace based on how much time is available. For example, if a section has 60 questions and the time limit is 30 minutes, you know you have to average 30 seconds or less per question in order to answer them all. Although 30 seconds is the hard limit, set 25 seconds per question as your goal, so you reserve extra time to spend on harder questions. When you budget extra time for the harder questions, you no longer have any reason to stress when those questions take longer to answer.

Don't let this time expectation distract you from working through the test at a calm, steady pace, but keep it in mind so you don't spend too much time on any one question. Recognize that taking extra time on one question you don't understand may keep you from answering two that you do understand later in the test. If your time limit for a question is up and you're still not sure of the answer, mark it and move on, and come back to it later if the time and the test format allow. If the testing format doesn't allow you to return to earlier questions, just make an educated guess; then put it out of your mind and move on.

On the easier questions, be careful not to rush. It may seem wise to hurry through them so you have more time for the challenging ones, but it's not worth missing one if you know the concept and just didn't take the time to read the question fully. Work efficiently but make sure you understand the question and have looked at all of the answer choices, since more than one may seem right at first.

Even if you're paying attention to the time, you may find yourself a little behind at some point. You should speed up to get back on track, but do so wisely. Don't panic; just take a few seconds less on each question until you're caught up. Don't guess without thinking, but do look through the answer choices and eliminate any you know are wrong. If you can get down to two choices, it is often worthwhile to guess from those. Once you've chosen an answer, move on and don't dwell on any that you skipped or had to hurry through. If a question was taking too long, chances are it was one of the harder ones, so you weren't as likely to get it right anyway.

On the other hand, if you find yourself getting ahead of schedule, it may be beneficial to slow down a little. The more quickly you work, the more likely you are to make a careless mistake that will affect your score. You've budgeted time for each question, so don't be afraid to spend that time. Practice an efficient but careful pace to get the most out of the time you have.

Secret Key #5 – Have a Plan for Guessing

When you're taking the test, you may find yourself stuck on a question. Some of the answer choices seem better than others, but you don't see the one answer choice that is obviously correct. What do you do?

The scenario described above is very common, yet most test takers have not effectively prepared for it. Developing and practicing a plan for guessing may be one of the single most effective uses of your time as you get ready for the exam.

In developing your plan for guessing, there are three questions to address:

- When should you start the guessing process?
- How should you narrow down the choices?
- Which answer should you choose?

When to Start the Guessing Process

Unless your plan for guessing is to select C every time (which, despite its merits, is not what we recommend), you need to leave yourself enough time to apply your answer elimination strategies. Since you have a limited amount of time for each question, that means that if you're going to give yourself the best shot at guessing correctly, you have to decide quickly whether or not you will guess.

Of course, the best-case scenario is that you don't have to guess at all, so first, see if you can answer the question based on your knowledge of the subject and basic reasoning skills. Focus on the key words in the question and try to jog your memory of related topics. Give yourself a chance to bring the knowledge to mind, but once you realize that you don't have (or you can't access) the knowledge you need to answer the question, it's time to start the guessing process.

It's almost always better to start the guessing process too early than too late. It only takes a few seconds to remember something and answer the question from knowledge. Carefully eliminating wrong answer choices takes longer. Plus, going through the process of eliminating answer choices can actually help jog your memory.

Summary: Start the guessing process as soon as you decide that you can't answer the question based on your knowledge.

How to Narrow Down the Choices

The next chapter in this book (**Test-Taking Strategies**) includes a wide range of strategies for how to approach questions and how to look for answer choices to eliminate. You will definitely want to read those carefully, practice them, and figure out which ones work best for you. Here though, we're going to address a mindset rather than a particular strategy.

Your odds of guessing an answer correctly depend on how many options you are choosing from.

Number of options left	5	4	3	2	1
Odds of guessing correctly	20%	25%	33%	50%	100%

You can see from this chart just how valuable it is to be able to eliminate incorrect answers and make an educated guess, but there are two things that many test takers do that cause them to miss out on the benefits of guessing:

- Accidentally eliminating the correct answer
- Selecting an answer based on an impression

We'll look at the first one here, and the second one in the next section.

To avoid accidentally eliminating the correct answer, we recommend a thought exercise called **the $5 challenge**. In this challenge, you only eliminate an answer choice from contention if you are willing to bet $5 on it being wrong. Why $5? Five dollars is a small but not insignificant amount of money. It's an amount you could afford to lose but wouldn't want to throw away. And while losing $5 once might not hurt too much, doing it twenty times will set you back $100. In the same way, each small decision you make—eliminating a choice here, guessing on a question there—won't by itself impact your score very much, but when you put them all together, they can make a big difference. By holding each answer choice elimination decision to a higher standard, you can reduce the risk of accidentally eliminating the correct answer.

The $5 challenge can also be applied in a positive sense: If you are willing to bet $5 that an answer choice *is* correct, go ahead and mark it as correct.

Summary: Only eliminate an answer choice if you are willing to bet $5 that it is wrong.

Which Answer to Choose

You're taking the test. You've run into a hard question and decided you'll have to guess. You've eliminated all the answer choices you're willing to bet $5 on. Now you have to pick an answer. Why do we even need to talk about this? Why can't you just pick whichever one you feel like when the time comes?

The answer to these questions is that if you don't come into the test with a plan, you'll rely on your impression to select an answer choice, and if you do that, you risk falling into a trap. The test writers know that everyone who takes their test will be guessing on some of the questions, so they intentionally write wrong answer choices to seem plausible. You still have to pick an answer though, and if the wrong answer choices are designed to look right, how can you ever be sure that you're not falling for their trap? The best solution we've found to this dilemma is to take the decision out of your hands entirely. Here is the process we recommend:

Once you've eliminated any choices that you are confident (willing to bet $5) are wrong, select the first remaining choice as your answer.

Whether you choose to select the first remaining choice, the second, or the last, the important thing is that you use some preselected standard. Using this approach guarantees that you will not be enticed into selecting an answer choice that looks right, because you are not basing your decision on how the answer choices look.

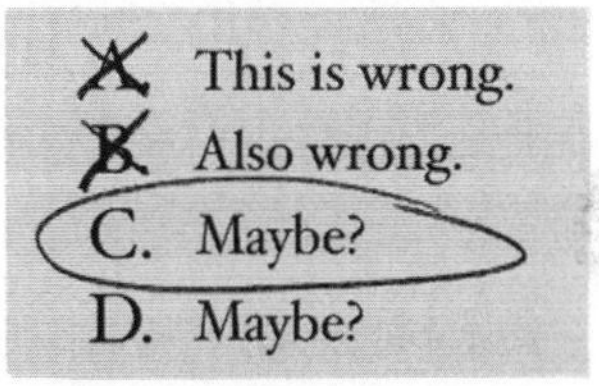

This is not meant to make you question your knowledge. Instead, it is to help you recognize the difference between your knowledge and your impressions. There's a huge difference between thinking an answer is right because of what you know, and thinking an answer is right because it looks or sounds like it should be right.

Summary: To ensure that your selection is appropriately random, make a predetermined selection from among all answer choices you have not eliminated.

Test-Taking Strategies

This section contains a list of test-taking strategies that you may find helpful as you work through the test. By taking what you know and applying logical thought, you can maximize your chances of answering any question correctly!

It is very important to realize that every question is different and every person is different: no single strategy will work on every question, and no single strategy will work for every person. That's why we've included all of them here, so you can try them out and determine which ones work best for different types of questions and which ones work best for you.

Question Strategies

☑ Read Carefully

Read the question and the answer choices carefully. Don't miss the question because you misread the terms. You have plenty of time to read each question thoroughly and make sure you understand what is being asked. Yet a happy medium must be attained, so don't waste too much time. You must read carefully and efficiently.

☑ Contextual Clues

Look for contextual clues. If the question includes a word you are not familiar with, look at the immediate context for some indication of what the word might mean. Contextual clues can often give you all the information you need to decipher the meaning of an unfamiliar word. Even if you can't determine the meaning, you may be able to narrow down the possibilities enough to make a solid guess at the answer to the question.

☑ Prefixes

If you're having trouble with a word in the question or answer choices, try dissecting it. Take advantage of every clue that the word might include. Prefixes can be a huge help. Usually, they allow you to determine a basic meaning. *Pre-* means before, *post-* means after, *pro-* is positive, *de-* is negative. From prefixes, you can get an idea of the general meaning of the word and try to put it into context.

☑ Hedge Words

Watch out for critical hedge words, such as *likely, may, can, often, almost, mostly, usually, generally, rarely*, and *sometimes*. Question writers insert these hedge phrases to cover every possibility. Often an answer choice will be wrong simply because it leaves no room for exception. Be on guard for answer choices that have definitive words such as *exactly* and *always*.

☑ Switchback Words

Stay alert for *switchbacks*. These are the words and phrases frequently used to alert you to shifts in thought. The most common switchback words are *but, although*, and *however*. Others include *nevertheless, on the other hand, even though, while, in spite of, despite*, and *regardless of*. Switchback words are important to catch because they can change the direction of the question or an answer choice.

⊘ Face Value

When in doubt, use common sense. Accept the situation in the problem at face value. Don't read too much into it. These problems will not require you to make wild assumptions. If you have to go beyond creativity and warp time or space in order to have an answer choice fit the question, then you should move on and consider the other answer choices. These are normal problems rooted in reality. The applicable relationship or explanation may not be readily apparent, but it is there for you to figure out. Use your common sense to interpret anything that isn't clear.

Answer Choice Strategies

⊘ Answer Selection

The most thorough way to pick an answer choice is to identify and eliminate wrong answers until only one is left, then confirm it is the correct answer. Sometimes an answer choice may immediately seem right, but be careful. The test writers will usually put more than one reasonable answer choice on each question, so take a second to read all of them and make sure that the other choices are not equally obvious. As long as you have time left, it is better to read every answer choice than to pick the first one that looks right without checking the others.

⊘ Answer Choice Families

An answer choice family consists of two (in rare cases, three) answer choices that are very similar in construction and cannot all be true at the same time. If you see two answer choices that are direct opposites or parallels, one of them is usually the correct answer. For instance, if one answer choice says that quantity *x* increases and another either says that quantity *x* decreases (opposite) or says that quantity *y* increases (parallel), then those answer choices would fall into the same family. An answer choice that doesn't match the construction of the answer choice family is more likely to be incorrect. Most questions will not have answer choice families, but when they do appear, you should be prepared to recognize them.

⊘ Eliminate Answers

Eliminate answer choices as soon as you realize they are wrong, but make sure you consider all possibilities. If you are eliminating answer choices and realize that the last one you are left with is also wrong, don't panic. Start over and consider each choice again. There may be something you missed the first time that you will realize on the second pass.

⊘ Avoid Fact Traps

Don't be distracted by an answer choice that is factually true but doesn't answer the question. You are looking for the choice that answers the question. Stay focused on what the question is asking for so you don't accidentally pick an answer that is true but incorrect. Always go back to the question and make sure the answer choice you've selected actually answers the question and is not merely a true statement.

⊘ Extreme Statements

In general, you should avoid answers that put forth extreme actions as standard practice or proclaim controversial ideas as established fact. An answer choice that states the "process should be used in certain situations, if..." is much more likely to be correct than one that states the "process should be discontinued completely." The first is a calm rational statement and doesn't even make a definitive, uncompromising stance, using a hedge word *if* to provide wiggle room, whereas the second choice is far more extreme.

☑ Benchmark

As you read through the answer choices and you come across one that seems to answer the question well, mentally select that answer choice. This is not your final answer, but it's the one that will help you evaluate the other answer choices. The one that you selected is your benchmark or standard for judging each of the other answer choices. Every other answer choice must be compared to your benchmark. That choice is correct until proven otherwise by another answer choice beating it. If you find a better answer, then that one becomes your new benchmark. Once you've decided that no other choice answers the question as well as your benchmark, you have your final answer.

☑ Predict the Answer

Before you even start looking at the answer choices, it is often best to try to predict the answer. When you come up with the answer on your own, it is easier to avoid distractions and traps because you will know exactly what to look for. The right answer choice is unlikely to be word-for-word what you came up with, but it should be a close match. Even if you are confident that you have the right answer, you should still take the time to read each option before moving on.

General Strategies

☑ Tough Questions

If you are stumped on a problem or it appears too hard or too difficult, don't waste time. Move on! Remember though, if you can quickly check for obviously incorrect answer choices, your chances of guessing correctly are greatly improved. Before you completely give up, at least try to knock out a couple of possible answers. Eliminate what you can and then guess at the remaining answer choices before moving on.

☑ Check Your Work

Since you will probably not know every term listed and the answer to every question, it is important that you get credit for the ones that you do know. Don't miss any questions through careless mistakes. If at all possible, try to take a second to look back over your answer selection and make sure you've selected the correct answer choice and haven't made a costly careless mistake (such as marking an answer choice that you didn't mean to mark). This quick double check should more than pay for itself in caught mistakes for the time it costs.

☑ Pace Yourself

It's easy to be overwhelmed when you're looking at a page full of questions; your mind is confused and full of random thoughts, and the clock is ticking down faster than you would like. Calm down and maintain the pace that you have set for yourself. Especially as you get down to the last few minutes of the test, don't let the small numbers on the clock make you panic. As long as you are on track by monitoring your pace, you are guaranteed to have time for each question.

☑ Don't Rush

It is very easy to make errors when you are in a hurry. Maintaining a fast pace in answering questions is pointless if it makes you miss questions that you would have gotten right otherwise. Test writers like to include distracting information and wrong answers that seem right. Taking a little extra time to avoid careless mistakes can make all the difference in your test score. Find a pace that allows you to be confident in the answers that you select.

☑ KEEP MOVING

Panicking will not help you pass the test, so do your best to stay calm and keep moving. Taking deep breaths and going through the answer elimination steps you practiced can help to break through a stress barrier and keep your pace.

Final Notes

The combination of a solid foundation of content knowledge and the confidence that comes from practicing your plan for applying that knowledge is the key to maximizing your performance on test day. As your foundation of content knowledge is built up and strengthened, you'll find that the strategies included in this chapter become more and more effective in helping you quickly sift through the distractions and traps of the test to isolate the correct answer.

Now that you're preparing to move forward into the test content chapters of this book, be sure to keep your goal in mind. As you read, think about how you will be able to apply this information on the test. If you've already seen sample questions for the test and you have an idea of the question format and style, try to come up with questions of your own that you can answer based on what you're reading. This will give you valuable practice applying your knowledge in the same ways you can expect to on test day.

Good luck and good studying!

Verbal Review

Rule Busters

Each problem provides you with some known information. These are the rules that you have to work with. Rule busters are choices that immediately clash with a rule and can be quickly ruled out.

Example:

John is sitting next to Bob.

This is a rule. Therefore any seating combination that does not have John sitting next to Bob is a rule buster, and is wrong! Quickly scan through the list of answer choices and eliminate all of those that have Bob and John sitting apart.

Example:

Mary is not sitting next to Bob.

Here is another rule. Quickly scan back through the answer choices and eliminate any that have Mary and Bob sitting together. For every rule that is given, quickly check and see if there are any answer choices that immediately "bust" the rule and eliminate them.

Symbology

Don't try to remember all of the information in your head. Sketch out the problem using the information provided. As much as possible, use symbols to represent the problem. Letters are great for abbreviation. Use a "M" as a symbol for a man, and a "W" as a symbol for a woman. Use the first letters in names to describe people. Therefore, John becomes "J" and Paul becomes "P". If the problem involves a seating or standing arrangement, use blanks to represent the possible seats. Then if a rule states that John is in the rightmost seat, put a "J" in the rightmost blank. Fill in as much information as you can using your symbols. Symbols will help you save time from writing the names out and will allow you to make fast and accurate diagrams of the problem.

Scratch Aides

Use your text booklet as scratch paper extensively. It's a great ally! If you finish the Analytical Reasoning section without scribbles throughout, you didn't take advantage of all of your potential resources. A good diagram or drawing of the problem described gives you a huge aid to solving the problem. Take advantage of it!

Be forewarned though, when creating your drawings, be efficient. Don't waste time filling in more information that you need. This is why symbols are great tools. They will save time and effort. Don't include useless information on your diagram or spend time making it "pretty". Fill in what you can quickly deduce. Focus on getting the bare essentials down on paper and spend your time more productively trying to solve the problem.

Tough Questions

If you are stumped on a problem or it appears too hard or too difficult, don't waste time. Move on! Remember though, if you can quickly check for obvious "rule busters" your chances of guessing correctly are greatly improved. Before you completely give up, at least check for the easy rule busters, which should knock out a couple of possible answers. Eliminate what you can and then guess at the remainder before moving on.

Face Value

Always accept the situation in the problem at face value. Don't read too much into it. The Wonderlic isn't trying to throw you off with a cheap trick. If it says there are six seats in a row, you can be confident that it is a single file row and one person is seated directly beside the next person and there are two ends to the row. Don't overcomplicate the problem by creating theoretical scenarios that will warp time or space. These are normal problems with solvable answers. It's just that all of the information isn't readily apparent and you have to figure things out.

Read Carefully

Understand what the problem is about. Read the description of the problem carefully. Don't miss the question because you misunderstood the explanation of the problem. The description is there because it is important in understanding the problem. Don't waste too much time though. You must read carefully and efficiently.

Danger Words

Some words go with a warning. They can be dangerous in any problem, not just Analytical Reasoning problems. These are "hedge" words such as the following: only, exactly, but, never, can be, cannot be, always, must be, least, most, highest, lowest, first, last, none, entire, all, no, unless, each, every. These words can completely alter the meaning of a sentence or a question and can easily be missed if you're reading quickly. Watch out!

Loose vs Tight

Rules are often either "loose" or "tight". Don't confuse the two when you check for rule breakers. A loose rule gives vague details about the problem. A tight rule gives specific details about the problem. Tight rules are much more helpful, providing more information, and allowing you to make clear determinations about answer choices more easily.

Example:

Loose: Bob is standing somewhere behind Joe.

Tight: Bob is standing directly behind Joe.

Don't mistakenly eliminate an answer choice that has Bob standing two spaces back from Joe, if only the loose rule above is given. If the loose rule is given, you can only eliminate answer choices that have Bob in front of Joe.

Double Negatives

A double negative can be treated as an affirmative. If a rule or answer choice has two negatives, mentally switch it to a single positive.

Example:

He is not going to not be there. = He is going to be there.

Answer Selection

Eliminate choices as soon as you realize they are wrong. But be careful! Make sure you consider all of the possible answer choices. Just because one appears right, doesn't mean that the next one won't be even better! Take a second to make sure that the other choices are not equally obvious. Don't make a hasty mistake. There are only two times that you should stop before checking other answers. First is when you are positive that the answer choice you have selected satisfies all of the rules. Second is when time is almost out and you have to make a quick guess!

The Wonderlic test will usually put more than one good answer choice for every question, so read all of them. Don't worry if you are stuck between two that seem right. By eliminating the other three your odds are now 50/50 if you have it down to two. Rather than wasting too much time, play the odds. You are guessing, but guessing wisely, because you've been able to knock out some of the answer choices that you know are wrong. If you are eliminating choices and realize that the answer choice you are left with is also obviously wrong, don't panic. Start over and consider each choice again. There may easily be something that you missed the first time and will realize on the second pass.

Common Sense

When in doubt, use common sense. These problems will not require you to make huge leaps of logic. If you think a leap of logic is necessary, read back through the set of conditions and question in order to gain a better understanding. Don't read too much into the question or set of conditions. Use your common sense to interpret anything that isn't clear. These are normal problems rooted in reality.

Final Notes

Some problems may have complicated reasoning that must be sorted through. Before you pick an answer choice and work it out in great detail, which takes a lot of time, first look briefly through the other answer choices to see if any of them are readily obvious as being correct. Always use your time efficiently. Don't panic, stay focused. Work systematically. Read the problem carefully. Eliminate the answer choices that are immediately wrong and are rule busters. Keep narrowing the search until you are either left with the answer or must guess at the answer from a more selective group of choices.

Mathematics Review

Most of the math problems on the Wonderlic are in the form of word problems. With word problems, the difficulty is rarely in performing the calculations themselves. Instead, the difficulty is in determining what calculations need to be performed, which typically involves translating the word problem into an equation or set of equations. The following sections will go over the computation skills and concepts you'll need for the test, but the more important skill is speed in interpreting the word problems. For that, there's nothing that will substitute for lots of practice.

Numbers and Their Classifications

Numbers are the basic building blocks of mathematics. Specific features of numbers are identified by the following terms:

Integers – The set of whole positive and negative numbers, including zero. Integers do not include fractions $\left(\frac{1}{3}\right)$, decimals (0.56), or mixed numbers $\left(7\frac{3}{4}\right)$.

Prime number – A whole number greater than 1 that has only two factors, itself and 1; that is, a number that can be divided evenly only by 1 and itself.

Composite number – A whole number greater than 1 that has more than two different factors; in other words, any whole number that is not a prime number. For example: The composite number 8 has the factors of 1, 2, 4, and 8.

Even number – Any integer that can be divided by 2 without leaving a remainder. For example: 2, 4, 6, 8, and so on.

Odd number – Any integer that cannot be divided evenly by 2. For example: 3, 5, 7, 9, and so on.

Decimal number – a number that uses a decimal point to show the part of the number that is less than one. Example: 1.234.

Decimal point – a symbol used to separate the ones place from the tenths place in decimals or dollars from cents in currency.

Decimal place – the position of a number to the right of the decimal point. In the decimal 0.123, the 1 is in the first place to the right of the decimal point, indicating tenths; the 2 is in the second place, indicating hundredths; and the 3 is in the third place, indicating thousandths.

The decimal, or base 10, system is a number system that uses ten different digits $(0, 1, 2, 3, 4, 5, 6, 7, 8, 9)$. An example of a number system that uses something other than ten digits is the binary, or base 2, number system, used by computers, which uses only the numbers 0 and 1. It is thought that the decimal system originated because people had only their 10 fingers for counting.

Rational, irrational, and real numbers can be described as follows:

Rational numbers include all integers, decimals, and fractions. Any terminating or repeating decimal number is a rational number.

Irrational numbers cannot be written as fractions or decimals because the number of decimal places is infinite and there is no recurring pattern of digits within the number. For example, pi (π) begins with 3.141592 and continues without terminating or repeating, so pi is an irrational number.

Real numbers are the set of all rational and irrational numbers.

Review Video: Classification of Numbers
Visit mometrix.com/academy and enter code: 461071

Review Video: Rational and Irrational Numbers
Visit mometrix.com/academy and enter code: 280645

Review Video: Prime and Composite Numbers
Visit mometrix.com/academy and enter code: 565581

Operations

There are four basic mathematical operations:

Addition increases the value of one quantity by the value of another quantity. Example: $2 + 4 = 6; 8 + 9 = 17$. The result is called the sum. With addition, the order does not matter. $4 + 2 = 2 + 4$.

Subtraction is the opposite operation to addition; it decreases the value of one quantity by the value of another quantity. Example: $6 - 4 = 2; 17 - 8 = 9$. The result is called the difference. Note that with subtraction, the order does matter. $6 - 4 \neq 4 - 6$.

Multiplication can be thought of as repeated addition. One number tells how many times to add the other number to itself. Example: 3×2 (three times two) $= 2 + 2 + 2 = 6$. With multiplication, the order does not matter. $2 \times 3 = 3 \times 2$ or $3 + 3 = 2 + 2 + 2$.

Division is the opposite operation to multiplication; one number tells us how many parts to divide the other number into. Example: $20 \div 4 = 5$; if 20 is split into 4 equal parts, each part is 5. With division, the order of the numbers does matter. $20 \div 4 \neq 4 \div 20$.

Review Video: Mathematical Operations
Visit mometrix.com/academy and enter code: 208095

An exponent is a superscript number placed next to another number at the top right. It indicates how many times the base number is to be multiplied by itself. Exponents provide a shorthand way to write what would be a longer mathematical expression. Example: $a^2 = a \times a$; $2^4 = 2 \times 2 \times 2 \times 2$. A number with an exponent of 2 is said to be "squared," while a number with an exponent of 3 is said to be "cubed." The value of a number raised to an exponent is called its power. So, 8^4 is read as "8 to the 4th power," or "8 raised to the power of 4." A negative exponent is the same as the reciprocal of a positive exponent. Example: $a^{-2} = \frac{1}{a^2}$.

Review Video: Exponents
Visit mometrix.com/academy and enter code: 600998

Parentheses are used to designate which operations should be done first when there are multiple operations. Example: 4 – (2 + 1) = 1; the parentheses tell us that we must add 2 and 1, and then subtract the sum from 4, rather than subtracting 2 from 4 and then adding 1 (this would give us an answer of 3).

Order of Operations is a set of rules that dictates the order in which we must perform each operation in an expression so that we will evaluate it accurately. If we have an expression that includes multiple different operations, Order of Operations tells us which operations to do first. The most common mnemonic for Order of Operations is PEMDAS, or "Please Excuse My Dear Aunt Sally." PEMDAS stands for Parentheses, Exponents, Multiplication, Division, Addition, Subtraction. It is important to understand that multiplication and division have equal precedence, as do addition and subtraction, so those pairs of operations are simply worked from left to right in order.

Example: Evaluate the expression $5 + 20 \div 4 \times (2 + 3)^2 - 6$ using the correct order of operations.

P: Perform the operations inside the parentheses, $(2 + 3) = 5$.

E: Simplify the exponents, $(5)^2 = 25$.

The equation now looks like this: $5 + 20 \div 4 \times 25 - 6$.

MD: Perform multiplication and division from left to right, $20 \div 4 = 5$; then $5 \times 25 = 125$.

The equation now looks like this: $5 + 125 - 6$.

AS: Perform addition and subtraction from left to right, $5 + 125 = 130$; then $130 - 6 = 124$.

Review Video: Order of Operations
Visit mometrix.com/academy and enter code: 259675

The laws of exponents are as follows:

1. Any number to the power of 1 is equal to itself: $a^1 = a$.
2. The number 1 raised to any power is equal to 1: $1^n = 1$.
3. Any number raised to the power of 0 is equal to 1: $a^0 = 1$.
4. Add exponents to multiply powers of the same base number:$a^n \times a^m = a^{n+m}$.
5. Subtract exponents to divide powers of the same number; that is $a^n \div a^m = a^{n-m}$.
6. Multiply exponents to raise a power to a power: $(a^n)^m = a^{n \times m}$.
7. If multiplied or divided numbers inside parentheses are collectively raised to a power, this is the same as each individual term being raised to that power: $(a \times b)^n = a^n \times b^n$; $(a \div b)^n = a^n \div b^n$.

Note: Exponents do not have to be integers. Fractional or decimal exponents follow all the rules above as well. Example: $5^{\frac{1}{4}} \times 5^{\frac{3}{4}} = 5^{\frac{1}{4}+\frac{3}{4}} = 5^1 = 5$.

A root, such as a square root, is another way of writing a fractional exponent. Instead of using a superscript, roots use the radical symbol ($\sqrt{\ }$) to indicate the operation. A radical will have a number underneath the bar, and may sometimes have a number in the upper left: $\sqrt[n]{a}$, read as "the nth root of a." The relationship between radical notation and exponent notation can be described by this equation: $\sqrt[n]{a} = a^{\frac{1}{n}}$. The two special cases of $n = 2$ and $n = 3$ are called square roots and cube roots. If there is no number to the upper left, it is understood to be a square root ($n = 2$). Nearly all of the roots you encounter will be square roots. A square root is the same as a number raised to the one-half power. When we say that a is the square root of b ($a = \sqrt{b}$), we mean that a multiplied by itself equals b: ($a \times a = b$).

A perfect square is a number that has an integer for its square root. There are 10 perfect squares from 1 to 100: 1, 4, 9, 16, 25, 36, 49, 64, 81, 100 (the squares of integers 1 through 10).

Scientific notation is a way of writing large numbers in a shorter form. The form $a \times 10^n$ is used in scientific notation, where a is greater than or equal to 1, but less than 10, and n is the number of places the decimal must move to get from the original number to a. Example: The number 230,400,000 is cumbersome to write. To write the value in scientific notation, place a decimal point between the first and second numbers, and include all digits through the last non-zero digit ($a = 2.304$). To find the appropriate power of 10, count the number of places the decimal point had to move ($n = 8$). The number is positive if the decimal moved to the left, and negative if it moved to the right. We can then write 230,400,000 as 2.304×10^8. If we look instead at the number 0.00002304, we have the same value for a, but this time the decimal moved 5 places to the right ($n = -5$). Thus, 0.00002304 can be written as 2.304×10^{-5}. Using this notation makes it simple to compare very large or very small numbers. By comparing exponents, it is easy to see that 3.28×10^4 is smaller than 1.51×10^5, because 4 is less than 5.

Review Video: Scientific Notation
Visit mometrix.com/academy and enter code: 976454

Positive and Negative Numbers

A precursor to working with negative numbers is understanding what **absolute values** are. A number's absolute value is simply the distance away from zero a number is on the number line. The absolute value of a number is always positive and is written $|x|$. For example, the absolute value of 3, written as $|3|$, is 3 because the distance between 0 and 3 on a number line is three units. Likewise, the absolute value of –3, written as $|-3|$, is 3 because the distance between 0 and –3 on a number line is three units. So $|3| = |-3|$.

Review Video: Absolute Value
Visit mometrix.com/academy and enter code: 314669

When adding signed numbers, if the signs are the same simply add the absolute values of the addends and apply the original sign to the sum. For example, $(+4) + (+8) = +12$ and $(-4) + (-8) = -12$. When the original signs are different, take the absolute values of the addends and subtract the smaller value from the larger value, then apply the original sign of the larger value to the difference. For instance, $(+4) + (-8) = -4$ and $(-4) + (+8) = +4$.

For subtracting signed numbers, change the sign of the number after the minus symbol and then follow the same rules used for addition. For example, $(+4) - (+8) = (+4) + (-8) = -4$.

If the signs are the same the product is positive when multiplying signed numbers. For example, $(+4) \times (+8) = +32$ and $(-4) \times (-8) = +32$. If the signs are opposite, the product is negative. For example, $(+4) \times (-8) = -32$ and $(-4) \times (+8) = -32$. When more than two factors are multiplied together, the sign of the product is determined by how many negative factors are present. If there are an odd number of negative factors then the product is negative, whereas an even number of negative factors indicates a positive product. For instance, $(+4) \times (-8) \times (-2) = +64$ and $(-4) \times (-8) \times (-2) = -64$.

The rules for dividing signed numbers are similar to multiplying signed numbers. If the dividend and divisor have the same sign, the quotient is positive. If the dividend and divisor have opposite signs, the quotient is negative. For example, $(-4) \div (+8) = -0.5$.

Factors and Multiples

Factors are numbers that are multiplied together to obtain a product. For example, in the equation $2 \times 3 = 6$, the numbers 2 and 3 are factors. A prime number has only two factors (1 and itself), but other numbers can have many factors.

A common factor is a number that divides exactly into two or more other numbers. For example, the factors of 12 are 1, 2, 3, 4, 6, and 12, while the factors of 15 are 1, 3, 5, and 15. The common factors of 12 and 15 are 1 and 3.

A prime factor is also a prime number. Therefore, the prime factors of 12 are 2 and 3. For 15, the prime factors are 3 and 5.

Review Video: Factors
Visit mometrix.com/academy and enter code: 920086

The greatest common factor (GCF) is the largest number that is a factor of two or more numbers. For example, the factors of 15 are 1, 3, 5, and 15; the factors of 35 are 1, 5, 7, and 35. Therefore, the greatest common factor of 15 and 35 is 5.

Review Video: Greatest Common Factor and Least Common Multiple
Visit mometrix.com/academy and enter code: 838699

The least common multiple (LCM) is the smallest number that is a multiple of two or more numbers. For example, the multiples of 3 include 3, 6, 9, 12, 15, etc.; the multiples of 5 include 5, 10, 15, 20, etc. Therefore, the least common multiple of 3 and 5 is 15.

Fractions, Percentages, and Related Concepts

A fraction is a number that is expressed as one integer written above another integer, with a dividing line between them ($\frac{x}{y}$). It represents the quotient of the two numbers "x divided by y." It can also be thought of as x out of y equal parts.

The top number of a fraction is called the numerator, and it represents the number of parts under consideration. The 1 in $\frac{1}{4}$ means that 1 part out of the whole is being considered in the calculation. The bottom number of a fraction is called the denominator, and it represents the total number of equal parts. The 4 in $\frac{1}{4}$ means that the whole consists of 4 equal parts. A fraction cannot have a denominator of zero; this is referred to as "undefined."

Review Video: Overview of Fractions
Visit mometrix.com/academy and enter code: 262335

Fractions can be manipulated, without changing the value of the fraction, by multiplying or dividing (but not adding or subtracting) both the numerator and denominator by the same number. If you divide both numbers by a common factor, you are reducing or simplifying the fraction. Two fractions that have the same value, but are expressed differently are known as equivalent fractions. For example, $\frac{2}{10}, \frac{3}{15}, \frac{4}{20}$, and $\frac{5}{25}$ are all equivalent fractions. They can also all be reduced or simplified to $\frac{1}{5}$.

When two fractions are manipulated so that they have the same denominator, this is known as finding a common denominator. The number chosen to be that common denominator should be the least common multiple of the two original denominators. Example: $\frac{3}{4}$ and $\frac{5}{6}$; the least common multiple of 4 and 6 is 12. Manipulating to achieve the common denominator: $\frac{3}{4} = \frac{9}{12}; \frac{5}{6} = \frac{10}{12}$.

If two fractions have a common denominator, they can be added or subtracted simply by adding or subtracting the two numerators and retaining the same denominator. Example: $\frac{1}{2} + \frac{1}{4} = \frac{2}{4} + \frac{1}{4} = \frac{3}{4}$. If the two fractions do not already have the same denominator, one or both of them must be manipulated to achieve a common denominator before they can be added or subtracted.

Review Video: Adding and Subtracting Fractions
Visit mometrix.com/academy and enter code: 378080

Two fractions can be multiplied by multiplying the two numerators to find the new numerator and the two denominators to find the new denominator. Example: $\frac{1}{3} \times \frac{2}{3} = \frac{1 \times 2}{3 \times 3} = \frac{2}{9}$.

Two fractions can be divided flipping the numerator and denominator of the second fraction and then proceeding as though it were a multiplication. Example: $\frac{2}{3} \div \frac{3}{4} = \frac{2}{3} \times \frac{4}{3} = \frac{8}{9}$.

Review Video: Multiplying and Dividing Fractions
Visit mometrix.com/academy and enter code: 473632

A fraction whose denominator is greater than its numerator is known as a proper fraction, while a fraction whose numerator is greater than its denominator is known as an improper fraction. Proper fractions have values less than one and improper fractions have values greater than one.

A mixed number is a number that contains both an integer and a fraction. Any improper fraction can be rewritten as a mixed number. Example: $\frac{8}{3} = \frac{6}{3} + \frac{2}{3} = 2 + \frac{2}{3} = 2\frac{2}{3}$. Similarly, any mixed number can be rewritten as an improper fraction. Example: $1\frac{3}{5} = 1 + \frac{3}{5} = \frac{5}{5} + \frac{3}{5} = \frac{8}{5}$.

Percentages can be thought of as fractions that are based on a whole of 100; that is, one whole is equal to 100%. The word percent means "per hundred." Fractions can be expressed as percents by finding equivalent fractions with a denomination of 100. Example: $\frac{7}{10} = \frac{70}{100} = 70\%; \frac{1}{4} = \frac{25}{100} = 25\%$.

To express a percentage as a fraction, divide the percentage number by 100 and reduce the fraction to its simplest possible terms. Example: $60\% = \frac{60}{100} = \frac{3}{5}; 96\% = \frac{96}{100} = \frac{24}{25}$.

Converting decimals to percentages and percentages to decimals is as simple as moving the decimal point. To convert from a decimal to a percent, move the decimal point two places to the right. To convert from a percent to a decimal, move it two places to the left. Example: 0.23 = 23%; 5.34 = 534%; 0.007 = 0.7%; 700% = 7.00; 86% = 0.86; 0.15% = 0.0015.

It may be helpful to remember that the percentage number will always be larger than the equivalent decimal number.

A percentage problem can be presented three main ways:

- Find what percentage of some number another number is.

  Example: What percentage of 40 is 8?

- Find what number is some percentage of a given number.

  Example: What number is 20% of 40?

- Find what number another number is a given percentage of.

  Example: What number is 8 20% of?

The three components in all of these cases are the same: a whole (W), a part (P), and a percentage (%). These are related by the equation: $P = W \times \%$. This is the form of the equation you would use to solve problems of type (2). To solve types (1) and (3), you would use these two forms: $\% = \frac{P}{W}$ and $W = \frac{P}{\%}$.

The thing that frequently makes percentage problems difficult is that they are most often also word problems, so a large part of solving them is figuring out which quantities are what. Example: In a school cafeteria, 7 students choose pizza, 9 choose hamburgers, and 4 choose tacos. Find the percentage that chooses tacos. To find the whole, you must first add all of the parts: 7 + 9 + 4 = 20. The percentage can then be found by dividing the part by the whole ($\% = \frac{P}{W}$): $\frac{4}{20} = \frac{20}{100} = 20\%$.

A ratio is a comparison of two quantities in a particular order. Example: If there are 14 computers in a lab, and the class has 20 students, there is a student to computer ratio of 20 to 14, commonly written as 20:14. Ratios are normally reduced to their smallest whole number representation, so 20:14 would be reduced to 10:7 by dividing both sides by 2.

Review Video: Ratios
Visit mometrix.com/academy and enter code: 996914

A proportion is a relationship between two quantities that dictates how one changes when the other changes. A direct proportion describes a relationship in which a quantity increases by a set amount for every increase in the other quantity, or decreases by that same amount for every decrease in the other quantity. Example: Assuming a constant driving speed, the time required for a car trip increases as the distance of the trip increases. The distance to be traveled and the time required to travel are directly proportional.

Review Video: Proportions
Visit mometrix.com/academy and enter code: 505355

Inverse proportion is a relationship in which an increase in one quantity is accompanied by a decrease in the other, or vice versa. Example: the time required for a car trip decreases as the speed increases, and increases as the speed decreases, so the time required is inversely proportional to the speed of the car.

Systems of Equations

Systems of Equations are a set of simultaneous equations that all use the same variables. A solution to a system of equations must be true for each equation in the system. *Consistent Systems* are those with at least one solution. *Inconsistent Systems* are systems of equations that have no solution.

To solve a system of linear equations by **substitution**, start with the easier equation and solve for one of the variables. Express this variable in terms of the other variable. Substitute this expression in the other equation and solve for the other variable. The solution should be expressed in the form (x, y). Substitute the values into both of the original equations to check your answer. Consider the following system of equations:

$$x + 6y = 15$$
$$3x - 12y = 18$$

Solving the first equation for x: $x = 15 - 6y$

Substitute this value in place of x in the second equation, and solve for y:

$$\begin{aligned} 3(15 - 6y) - 12y &= 18 \\ 45 - 18y - 12y &= 18 \\ 30y &= 27 \\ y &= \frac{27}{30} = \frac{9}{10} = 0.9 \end{aligned}$$

Plug this value for y back into the first equation to solve for x:

$$x = 15 - 6(0.9) = 15 - 5.4 = 9.6$$

Check both equations if you have time:

$$\begin{aligned} 9.6 + 6(0.9) &= 15 \\ 9.6 + 5.4 &= 15 \\ 15 &= 15 \end{aligned} \qquad \begin{aligned} 3(9.6) - 12(0.9) &= 18 \\ 28.8 - 10.8 &= 18 \\ 18 &= 18 \end{aligned}$$

Therefore, the solution is (9.6,0.9).

Review Video: The Substitution Method
Visit mometrix.com/academy and enter code: 565151

To solve a system of equations using *elimination*, begin by rewriting both equations in standard form $Ax + By = C$. Check to see if the coefficients of one pair of like variables add to zero. If not, multiply one or both of the equations by a non-zero number to make one set of like variables add to zero. Add the two equations to solve for one of the variables. Substitute this value into one of the original equations to solve for the other variable. Check your work by substituting into the other equation.

Next we will solve the same problem as above, but using the addition method.

Solve the system using elimination:

$$x + 6y = 15$$

$$3x - 12y = 18$$

If we multiply the first equation by 2, we can eliminate the y terms:

$$2x + 12y = 30$$

$$3x - 12y = 18$$

Add the equations together and solve for x:

$5x = 48$

$$x = \frac{48}{5} = 9.6$$

Plug the value for x back into either of the original equations and solve for y:

$9.6 + 6y = 15$

$$y = \frac{15 - 9.6}{6} = 0.9$$

Check both equations if you have time:

$$9.6 + 6(0.9) = 9.6 + 5.4 = 15$$

$$3(9.6) - 12(0.9) = 28.8 - 10.8 = 18$$

Therefore, the solution is (9.6, 0.9).

Review Video: Solving Linear Equations
Visit mometrix.com/academy and enter code: 746745

Review Video: Substitution and Elimination for Solving Linear Systems
Visit mometrix.com/academy and enter code: 958611

Polynomial Algebra

To multiply two binomials, follow the *FOIL* method. FOIL stands for:

- First: Multiply the first term of each binomial
- Outer: Multiply the outer terms of each binomial
- Inner: Multiply the inner terms of each binomial
- Last: Multiply the last term of each binomial

Using FOIL, $(Ax + By)(Cx + Dy) = ACx^2 + ADxy + BCxy + BDy^2$.

Review Video: Polynomials
Visit mometrix.com/academy and enter code: 305005

Special Report: Wonderlic Secrets in Action

Sample Math Question:

Three coins are tossed up in the air. What is the probability that two of them will land heads and one will land tails?

A. 0

B. 1/8

C. 1/4

D. 3/8

Let's look at a few different methods and steps to solving this problem.

1. Reduction and Division

Quickly eliminate the probabilities that you immediately know. You know to roll all heads is a 1/8 probability, and to roll all tails is a 1/8 probability. Since there are in total 8/8 probabilities, you can subtract those two out, leaving you with 8/8 - 1/8 - 1/8 = 6/8. So after eliminating the possibilities of getting all heads or all tails, you're left with 6/8 probability. Because there are only three coins, all other combinations are going to involve one of either head or tail, and two of the other. All other combinations will either be 2 heads and 1 tail, or 2 tails and 1 head. Those remaining combinations both have the same chance of occurring, meaning that you can just cut the remaining 6/8 probability in half, leaving you with a 3/8ths chance that there will be 2 heads and 1 tail, and another 3/8ths chance that there will be 2 tails and 1 head, making choice D correct.

2. Run Through the Possibilities for that Outcome

You know that you have to have two heads and one tail for the three coins. There are only so many combinations, so quickly run through them all.

You could have:

H, H, H

H, H, T

H, T, H

T, H, H

T, T, H

T, H, T

H, T, T

T, T, T

Reviewing these choices, you can see that three of the eight have two heads and one tail, making choice D correct.

3. Fill in the Blanks with Symbology and Odds

Many probability problems can be solved by drawing blanks on a piece of scratch paper (or making mental notes) for each object used in the problem, then filling in probabilities and multiplying them out. In this case, since there are three coins being flipped, draw three blanks. In the first blank, put an "H" and over it write "1/2". This represents the case where the first coin is flipped as heads. In that case (where the first coin comes up heads), one of the other two coins must come up tails and one must come up heads to fulfill the criteria posed in the problem (2 heads and 1 tail). In the second blank, put a "1" or "1/1". This is because it doesn't matter what is flipped for the second coin, so long as the first coin is heads. In the third blank, put a "1/2". This is because the third coin must be the exact opposite of whatever is in the second blank. Half the time the third coin will be the same as the second coin, and half the time the third coin will be the opposite, hence the "1/2". Now multiply out the odds. There is a half chance that the first coin will come up "heads", then it doesn't matter for the second coin, then there is a half chance that the third coin will be the opposite of the second coin, which will give the desired result of 2 heads and 1 tail. So, that gives 1/2*1/1*1/2 = 1/4.

But, now you must calculate the probabilities that result if the first coin is flipped tails. So draw another group of three blanks. In the first blank, put a "T" and over it write "1/2". This represents the case where the first coin is flipped as tails. In that case (where the first coin comes up tails), both of the other two coins must come up heads to fulfill the criteria posed in the problem. In the second blank, put an "H" and over it write "1/2". In the third blank, put an "H" and over it write "1/2". Now multiply out the odds. There is a half chance that the first coin will come up "tails", then there is a half chance that the second coin will be heads, and a half chance that the third coin will be heads. So, that gives 1/2*1/2*1/2 = 1/8.

Now, add those two probabilities together. If you flip heads with the first coin, there is a 1/4 chance of ultimately meeting the problem's criteria. If you flip tails with the first coin, there is a 1/8 chance of ultimately meeting the problem's criteria. So, that gives 1/4 + 1/8 = 2/8 + 1/8 = 3/8, which makes choice D correct.

Practice Test #1

Want to take this practice test in an online interactive format?
Check out the online resources page, which includes interactive practice questions and much more: **mometrix.com/resources719/wonderlicwptq**

1. **REFRAIN** **RECUSE**

These words have:

a. Similar meanings
b. Contradictory meanings
c. Neither similar nor contradictory meanings

2. Look at the row of numbers below. What number should come next?

10 20 15 30 25 50 ?

a. 35
b. 40
c. 45
d. 100

3. Assume the first two statements are true.

1. The girl plays outside every day
2. The weather is sometimes snowy
3. The girl is sometimes snowed upon

The third statement is:

a. True
b. False
c. Not certain

4. If it takes 1.5 hours to fly from city A to city B, and it takes 9 hours to fly from city A to city C, how much greater is the distance between cities A and C than the distance between cities A and B?

a. Two times as great
b. Four times as great
c. Six times as great
d. Seven-and-a-half times as great

5. If the first day of May is a Friday, what day will the 27th fall on?

a. Tuesday
b. Wednesday
c. Thursday
d. Friday

6. How many of the five pairs of names listed below are exact duplicates?

M.K. Fisher	M.K. Fischer
J.S. Waters	J.C. Waters
A.C. Thule	A.C. Thule
E.L. Petersen	E.L. Peterson
L.B. Baird	L.B. Baird

7. Owen and James start work at a company at the same time. Owen earns twice as much as James at first, but he does not receive a raise for five years, while James receives a $5,000 raise every year. After five years, their salaries are equal. How much did James make when they started working?

a. $5,000
b. $25,000
c. $50,000
d. $100,000

8. **RETRACT** **RETRIEVE**

These words have:

a. Similar meanings
b. Contradictory meanings
c. Neither similar nor contradictory meanings

9. Look at the row of numbers below. Which number is the smallest?

2 0.2 1/2 0.02 1/20

10. Lumber is on sale for 50% off the regular price. Rebecca purchases 5 meters of lumber for $12.50. What is the regular price per meter of lumber?

a. $2.50
b. $5.00
c. $15.00
d. $17.50

11. **REPORT** **REPRESS**

These words have:

a. Similar meanings
b. Contradictory meanings
c. Neither similar nor contradictory meanings

12. The numbers in the figures below have the same mathematical relationship to one another.

What number should replace the question mark in the figure below?

a. 0
b. 2
c. 6
d. 10

13. Assume the following two statements are true:

All students are required to take a math class before they graduate.
Sharon is a student.

Which of the following statements could be logically concluded?

a. Sharon is required to take a math class
b. Sharon is not a student
c. Sharon is not required to take a math class
d. Sharon is currently taking a math class

14. Define the value of a word as the sum of all letters, if each letter is replaced by a number representing its position in the alphabet. For example, the value of "cab" is 6, because C (3) + A (1) + B (2) = 6.

What is the value of the word "egg"?

a. 15
b. 17
c. 19
d. 21

15. Which month of the year contains the *fewest* hours of daylight in the Northern Hemisphere?

a. January
b. July
c. October
d. December

16. Assume the first two statements are true.

1. All employees must submit time sheets weekly
2. Mike is an employee
3. Mike has submitted this week's time sheet

The third statement is:

a. True
b. False
c. Not certain

17. Widgets sell for 50 cents each, for sales of up to 2,000 widgets. After that, the price drops to 25 cents each for all sales of more than 2,000 widgets. A customer pays $1,500 for his widget order. How many widgets has he ordered?

a. 1,000
b. 2,000
c. 3,000
d. 4,000

18. **CONFOUND** **CONFUSE**

These words have:

a. Similar meanings
b. Contradictory meanings
c. Neither similar nor contradictory meanings

19. Which of the following figures is most different from the others?

a. b. c. d.

20. A woman needs to replace the tires on her car. Brand A costs $500 and will last for 50,000 miles. Brand B costs $400 and will last for 40,000 miles. Which brand offers the best value based on miles per dollar?

a. Brand A
b. Brand B
c. Both offer equal value

21. Which word does not fit in the following list?

revive resume revert renew

22. Look at the row of numbers below. Which number is the smallest?

1/3 3 0.3 3/100 0.003

23. Assume the first two statements are true.

1. Joe and Sally know one another
2. Sally and Ian know one another
3. Joe and Ian know one another

The third statement is:

a. True
b. False
c. Not certain

24. Two people leave a city at the same time. One person travels at 30 miles an hour and arrives three hours later at his destination. The second person travels to a city 120 miles away and arrives at the same time. How fast is the second person traveling?

a. 30 miles an hour
b. 40 miles an hour
c. 50 miles an hour
d. 60 miles an hour

25. The officer cited the man for reckless driving, saying that he had failed to <u>heed</u> the signs about dangerous weather conditions.

In this context, <u>heed</u> most nearly means:

a. Obey
b. Ignore
c. See

26. Which of the following words contains the greatest number of *different* letters?

a. Abracadabra
b. Onomatopoeia
c. Disillusionment

27. A man is 1.5 times as old as his sister. He is now 30 years old. How old was he when she was born?

a. 5
b. 10
c. 15
d. 20

28. Which word does not fit in the following list?

inspire regret outrage provoke

29. Which of the following figures is most different from the others?

a.

b.

c.

d.

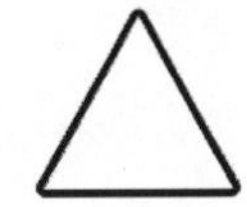

30. Plants are sold for $6 each. If a customer buys more than ten plants, the price drops to $5 for each plant after the tenth. How much will a customer pay for 15 plants?

a. $75
b. $85
c. $90
d. $100

Answer Key and Explanations for Test #1

1. A: have similar meanings. Both "to refrain" and "to recuse" refer to choosing not to participate in an activity.

2. C: The series of numbers is formed by performing two operations: doubling the first number to get the second, and then subtracting 5 to get the next, and repeating this pattern. Since 50 is 25 doubled, the next operation is to subtract 5, resulting in 45.

3. A: true. If the girl plays outside every day and the weather is sometimes snowy, then she will be playing outside on days it is snowy and will be snowed upon.

4. C: six times as far. Nine divided by 1.5 equals 6, so city C is six times farther from city A than city B is.

5. B: a Wednesday. There are seven days in a week, so adding multiples of 7 to 1 (for the first of the month) will find the other Fridays in the month. The other Fridays will be the 8th, the 15th, the 22nd, and the 29th. The 27th will be two days before Friday the 29th, meaning it will fall on a Wednesday.

6. Two are exact duplicates, A.C. Thule and L.B. Baird. In the first pair, Fisher is spelled differently from Fischer. In the second pair, the initials are J.S. and J.C. In the fourth pair, Petersen and Peterson are spelled differently.

7. B: $25,000. If James receives a $5,000 raise every year for five years, he has gained an income increase of $25,000. If their salaries are now equal, and James's salary was initially one-half of Owen's, then James has doubled his salary. Therefore, James initially earned $25,000.

8. A: have similar meanings. Both words involve taking something back; "to retract" something is to draw it back or withdraw it (for instance, a statement), and "to retrieve" something can mean to get it back or regain it.

9. 0.02: To find the answer, reformat all the numbers so they can be more easily compared. Since the list contains one fraction, change it to a decimal, and extend all numbers to two decimal places. Reformatting our list, we get

2.00 0.20 0.50 0.02 0.05

Now it is easy to see that 0.02 is the smallest number in the list.

10. B: $5.00. Rebecca purchased 5 meters of lumber for $12.50, so we simply divide $12.50 by 5 to find the sale price for one meter. 12.5 divided by 5 equals 2.5, so the sale price per meter is $2.50. The regular price is twice the sale price since the sale price is a 50% discount, so the regular price is $5.00 per meter.

11. B: have contradictory meanings. "To report" involves the disclosure of information, while "to repress" involves withholding it or preventing it from being disclosed.

12. D: 10. The numbers in the bottom boxes are exactly twice the number diagonal to them in the top boxes. In the example, $1 \times 2 = 2$ in the first figure, $2 \times 2 = 4$ and $3 \times 2 = 6$ in the second figure, and 0 × 2 = 0 and −1 × 2 = −2 in the third figure. In the question, we see that 3 × 2 = 6, just as in the example, so we should multiply 5 by 2 to get the missing answer, which is 10.

13. A: "Sharon is required to take a math class." B, "Sharon is not a student" is contradicted by the information we have already been given. C, "Sharon is not required to take a math class" cannot be true if all students are required to take a math class. D, "Sharon is currently taking a math class" is possibly, but not necessarily, true. She must take a math class at some point while she is a student, but we do not know that she is taking one now.

14. C: 19. First, count the letters of the alphabet to see what number represents each letter. E is the fifth letter of the alphabet, and G is the seventh. There are two Gs and one E in "egg," so, doing the math, we get (2 × 7) + 5 = 19.

15. D: December. The fewest hours of daylight occur at the start of winter, which is mid-December in the Northern Hemisphere. January, July, and October all have more hours of daylight.

16. C: not certain. We know that Mike must submit a time sheet weekly, since he is an employee, but we do not know that he has submitted this week's time sheet yet. It is possible, but not necessarily true, that he has done so already.

17. D: 4,000. First, find out how much the man would pay for 2,000 widgets. 2,000 × 0.50 = $1,000. He has paid more than that, so put that 2,000 figure aside and figure out how many more widgets he has bought than 2,000. He has paid $500 more at the lower rate. Dividing $500 by 0.25 gets us 2,000. Add back in the original 2,000 widgets he bought at the higher rate, and we see that he has bought 4,000 widgets in total.

18. A: have similar meanings. Both words are nearly synonymous, meaning to bewilder someone or misidentify two things as being the same.

19. D: All three of the other shapes have exactly five sides, while D has four sides. Other factors to consider might be whether the sides are all the same length, and whether all the angles are convex, or outward facing, but in both cases, there is more than one figure that breaks that pattern. The number of sides is the only characteristic where exactly one figure breaks the pattern.

20. C: both offer equal value. To compare these figures, simply divide the miles by the dollars to get the mile-per-dollar value. 50,000 ÷ $500 = 100, and 40,000 ÷ $400 = 100. Both offer a rate of 100 miles per dollar, so they are of equal value.

21. Revert: Revive, resume, and renew all use the "re-" prefix in the sense of repeating or doing something again. To "revive" is to bring to life again or to become alive again, to "resume" is to assume again or take up again, and to "renew" is to make new again. To "revert," however, uses the re- prefix in the sense of backward movement; i.e., going back to a previous state.

22. 0.003: To find the answer, reformat all numbers so they can be more easily compared. Since the list contains two fractions, change them to decimals, and extend all numbers to three decimal places. Reformatting our list, we get

0.333 3.000 0.300 0.030 0.003

Now it is easy to see that 0.003 is the smallest number in the list.

23. C: not certain. Joe and Sally know one another, and Sally knows Ian, but it does not follow that Joe and Ian must know one another. They may, or they may not, but their relationship with Sally does not determine whether they know one another or not.

24. B: 40 miles an hour. If the second person takes three hours to drive to a city 120 miles away, dividing 120 by 3 gets us 40 miles per hour.

25. A: obey. While it is possible that the man could fail to see the sign about dangerous weather conditions, the fact that the judge cites him for reckless driving suggests that he did see the sign but chose not to follow it.

26. C: disillusionment. "abracadabra" contains five unique letters, "onomatopoeia" contains eight, and "disillusionment" contains ten.

27. B: 10. This question is solved in two steps. First, we figure out how old the man's sister is. If he is 30, and he is 1.5 times as old as she is now, dividing 30 by 1.5 gets us 20. If she is 20 and he is 30, when she was born (i.e., when she was 0 years old), he was 10, which we get by subtracting her current age from his current age.

28. Regret: All three other verbs can refer to creating an effect on someone else, whereas regret is an internal emotion.

29. C: In the other three figures, all sides are the same length, but in figure C, the bottom side is shorter than the other two sides. Other things to consider might be the number of sides in each figure, but since two figures have three sides, we can dismiss that idea.

30. B: $85. First, figure out what buying 10 plants will cost the customer. At $6 each, 10 plants will cost $60, because 10 × 6 = 60. Subtract 10 from 15 to see how many plants they are buying at the lower rate, and we get 5. If the lower rate is $5, and the customer buys 5, they spend an additional $25. $25 + $60 = $85.

Practice Test #2

1. An elevator leaves the first floor of a 25-story building with 3 people on board. It stops at every floor. Each time it comes to an even-numbered floor, 3 people get on and one person gets off. Each time it comes to an odd-numbered floor, 3 people get on and 4 people get off. How many people are on board when it arrives at the 25th floor?

a. 13
b. 16
c. 15
d. 12

2. Which word does not belong with the others?

a. Artificial
b. Synthetic
c. Natural
d. Man-made

3. The bowl of change on your dresser totals $2.17. Which combination of coins could NOT be in the bowl?

a. 8 quarters, 1 dime, 1 nickel, and 2 pennies
b. 192 pennies and 1 quarter
c. 25 nickels, 11 dimes, and 2 pennies
d. 6 quarters, 6 dimes, 1 nickel, and 2 pennies

4. Choose the meaning of the underlined word.

The group hiked along a <u>precipitous</u> slope that many found unnerving.

a. rugged
b. dangerous
c. steep
d. wet

5. If 12 is added to the product of 13 and 7, the result is

a. 32
b. 79
c. 103
d. 240

6. Bernie arrived late for the performance. Tom arrived before Darius. Tom arrived after Bernie. If the first two statements are true, then the third is:

a. True
b. False
c. Unknown

7. What number is one half the average of 3, 4, and 5?

a. 1.5
b. 2
c. 4
d. 2.5

8. What is the mode of the following numbers: 14, 17, 14, 12, 13, 15, 22, 11?

a. 13.5
b. 14
c. 14.75
d. 16.5

9. A music download takes 15 minutes for the first 20%. If it continues at the same rate, what will be the total amount of time required to download the entire piece of music?

a. 1 hour 15 minutes
b. 1 hour
c. 50 minutes
d. 45 minutes

10. Multiplying a number by ⅔ is the same as dividing that same number by

a. ⅔
b. 3
c. 1
d. 3/2

11. Choose the meaning of the underlined word.

Stanley was so <u>besotted</u> with his prom date that he spent most of the dance gazing at her adoringly.

a. infatuated
b. infuriated
c. perplexed
d. engrossed

12. What number added to 23 makes a number equal to one half of 94?

a. 21
b. 23
c. 24
d. 26

13. On his last math test, Sam got 2 questions correct for every 3 questions he missed. If the test had a total of 60 questions, how many questions did Sam answer correctly?

a. 12
b. 24
c. 36
d. 60

14. What two numbers should come next in the series 1, 1, 2, 3, 5, 8, 13, ...?

a. 18, 24
b. 20, 28
c. 21, 29
d. 21, 34

15. Ellie was born one minute after Dean. Dean was born before Rob. Rob was born after Ellie. If the first two statements are true, then the third is:

a. True
b. False
c. Unknown

16. Put the following integers in order from greatest to least:

-52, 16, -12, 14, 8, -5, 0

a. -52, 16, -12, 14, 8, -5, 0
b. 0, -5, 8, -12, 14, 16, -52
c. 0, -5, -12, -52, 8, 14, 16
d. -52, -12, -5, 0, 8, 14, 16

17. Which of the following figures has rotational symmetry?

a. 
b. 
c. 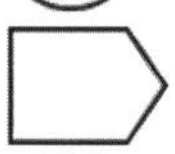
d. 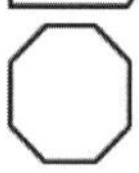

18. If an odd number is added to an even number, the result must be

a. odd
b. even
c. positive
d. zero

19. If number *x* is subtracted from 27, the result is -5. What is number *x*?

a. 22
b. 25
c. 32
d. 35

20. The ratio of blue food coloring to yellow food coloring used in making green cake frosting is 3 to 2. If 18 drops of blue food coloring are used, how many drops of yellow food coloring are needed?

a. 2
b. 6
c. 8
d. 12

21. What geometric figure is this?

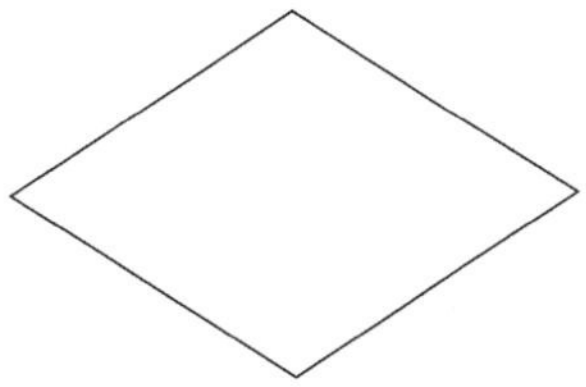

a. rhombus
b. trapezoid
c. pentagon
d. square

22. A combination lock uses a 3-digit code. Each digit can be any one of the ten available integers 0-9. How many different combinations are possible?

a. 9
b. 1,000
c. 81
d. 100

23. During the month of November, the Jones family spent $106.20 on fuel costs for their home. What was the average cost per day?

a. $3.43
b. $3.54
c. $5.31
d. $15.17

24. Richard buys two cups of coffee every day except Saturday and Sunday. On Saturday he buys only one cup, and on Sunday he buys none. If a cup of coffee costs $2.25, how much does Richard spend on coffee every week?

a. $25.00
b. $23.50
c. $24.75
d. $25.25

25. A shipping clerk can process 180 orders per hour. He has an assistant who can process 180 orders in 90 minutes. How many minutes will it take the two of them, working together, to process 115 orders?

a. 36
b. 23
c. 27
d. 30

26. Mackenzie left the daycare right after Austin. Nora left right before Austin. Mackenzie left before Austin. If the first two statements are true, then the third is:

a. True
b. False
c. Unknown

27. Choose the meaning of the underlined word.

Saline is taking a philosophy class but finds most of the readings to be very <u>obscure</u>, so she has not benefited much from them.

a. opinionated
b. unclear
c. offensive
d. benign

28. Which number could fill in the blank in this sequence? 1, 6, 16, __, 51

a. 31
b. 26
c. 41
d. 21

29. Which word does not belong with the others?

a. Painter
b. Artist
c. Musician
d. Dancer

30. Shun means the *opposite* of

a. Return
b. Embrace
c. Manipulate
d. Retract

Answer Key and Explanations for Test #2

1. B: There are 12 even-numbered floors between floors 1 and 25. At each one, the elevator gains 2 people, for a net gain of 24. There are 11 odd-numbered floors between floors 1 and 25 (not counting floors 1 and 25). At each one, the elevator loses 1 person, for a net loss of 11. The elevator leaves the first floor with 3 people, so the total arriving at the 25th floor is 3 + 24 – 11 = 16.

2. C: Natural is the opposite of the other words in the series. Artificial, synthetic, and man-made are all words for non-natural processes.

3. C: This combination of coins totals $2.37.

4. C: The word "precipitous" means "steep."

5. C: The product is the result of multiplying two numbers.

The product of 13 x 7 = 91. Add 12 to get 103, Choice C.

6. C: We can diagram this sentence as follows: Tom > Darius, which tells us that Tom arrived before Darius. We do not have enough information to determine when Bernie arrived in relation to the other two people.

7. B: To compute the average, first find the sum of all the items in the list and then divide by the number of items in the list. This yields $\frac{3+4+5}{3}=\frac{12}{3}=4$. One half of 4 is 2.

8. B: The mode is the value of the term that occurs most. Of these terms, the number 14 occurs twice, so Choice B is the correct answer.

9. A: Since 20% is equivalent to 1/5, it will take 5 times as long to download the entire piece of music. 5 x 15 = 75 minutes, this is equivalent to 1 hour 15 minutes.

10. D: Division is the opposite, or the reciprocal, of multiplication.

The reciprocal of ⅔ is $^3/_2$, Choice D.

11. A: Besotted means infatuated.

12. C: One half of 94 equals 47. Since 47 – 23 = 24, C is the correct answer.

13. B: The ratio of correct to incorrect answers is 2:3, giving a whole of 5. It takes 12 sets of 5 questions to total 60 questions. To determine how many correct answers Sam gave, multiply 2 by 12, for a total of 24, Choice B.

14. D: In this series, each number is the sum of the two preceding numbers. For example, 3 = 1 + 2, and 5 = 3 + 2. Therefore, the number following 13 must be 13 + 8 = 21, and the next number must be 21 + 13 = 34.

15. C: We can diagram this sentence as follows: Dean > Ellie; Dean > Rob. In other words, Dean was born before Ellie and before Rob. We do not have enough information to determine whether Ellie > Rob is true.

16. D: Think of the numbers as they would be on a number line to place them in the correct order.

17. D: Rotational symmetry is defined as a figure that looks exactly the same after being rotated any amount. Answer choice D is the only example given that would stay the same if rotated.

18. A: An odd number can be considered as an even number *N* plus 1. Two even numbers added together produce an even number, so the result of adding an odd and an even number must be an even number plus 1, which is odd. For example, 4 + 3 = 7.

19. C: In this problem, if you do not know how to solve, try filling in the answer choices to see which one checks out. Many math problems may be solved by a guess and check method when you have a selection of answer choices.

$27 - x = -5$

$x = 32$

20. D: Set up and solve a proportion. To solve the proportion, cross-multiply:

3 = 2

18 x

3x = 36

x = 12, Choice D.

21. A: A rhombus is four-sided polygon having all four sides of equal length. The sum of the angles of a rhombus is 360 degrees.

22. B: In this probability problem there are three independent events (the codes for each digit), each with ten possible outcomes (the numerals 0-9). Since the events are independent, the total possible outcomes equals the product of the possible outcomes for each of the three events, that is $P = P_1 \times P_2 \times P_3 = 10 \times 10 \times 10 = 1{,}000$

23. B: The average cost for the month is calculated by dividing the total cost ($106.20) by 30 (the number of days in November).

24. C: Since he buys two cups per day for five days, and one cup on Saturday, the total number of cups that Richard buys each week is (2 x 5) + 1 = 11 cups. Since each cup costs $2.25, the amount he spends is 11 x $2.25 = $24.75.

25. B: At 180 orders per hour, the clerk processes 3 orders per minute, since there are 60 minutes in an hour ($\frac{180}{60} = 3$). His assistant processes 2 orders per minute ($\frac{180}{90} = 2$). Together, they can process 3 + 2 = 5 orders per minute. Therefore, 115 orders will take $\frac{115}{5} = 23$ minutes.

26. B: We can diagram the first two sentences as follows: Mackenzie > Austin; Nora > Austin. The third sentence, which we could diagram as Mackenzie < Austin, contradicts the first sentence.

27. B: The word "obscure" means "unclear" and "difficult to understand."

28. A: The sequence increases by multiples of 5: to get from 1 to 6, add 5. To get from 6 to 16, add 10. To get from 16 to 31, add 15. To get from 31 to 51, add 20.

29. B: "Artist" is the general category that all the other items in the series belong to; painters, musicians, and dancers are all kinds of artists.

30. B: Shun means reject or ignore, the opposite of embrace.

Practice Test #3

1. The gardeners planted the sapling several yards from the other trees in order to <u>accommodate</u> the tree's future growth.

In this context, <u>accommodate</u> most nearly means:

a. Host
b. Allow
c. Restrict

2. Look at the row of numbers below.

27 9 3 1 ?

What number should come next?

a. 0
b. 3
c. 1/3
d. 1/9

3. Assume the following two statements are true:

All children must be vaccinated before being allowed to attend school.
Miguel does not attend school.

Which of the following statements could be logically concluded?

a. Miguel has been vaccinated
b. Miguel has not been vaccinated
c. Miguel is not allowed to attend school
d. None of these can be logically concluded

4. A certain recipe for a dozen cookies requires 3/4 of a cup of flour. To triple the recipe, how much flour would a cook require?

a. 2 1/4 cups
b. 2 1/2 cups
c. 2 3/4 cups
d. 3 cups

5. The seventh month of the year is:

a. July
b. August
c. September
d. October

6. Observe the following shape:

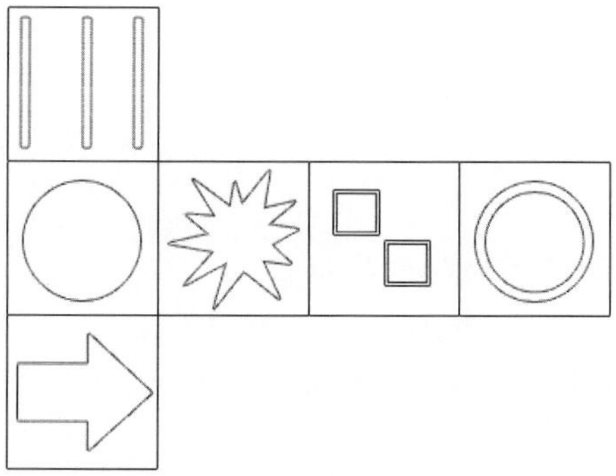

If this shape were folded into a cube, which of the following could result?

a. 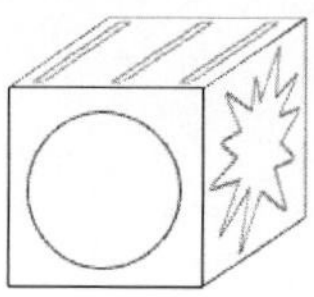

b. 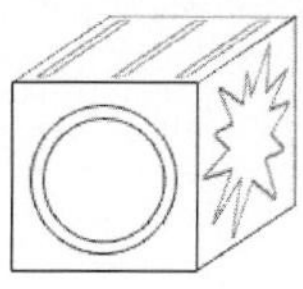

c. 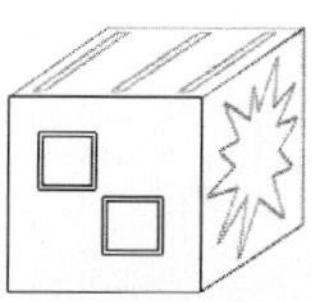

d. 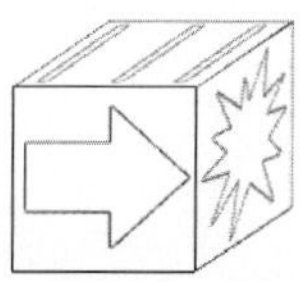

7. What percentage is equal to 0.75?

a. 75%
b. 750%
c. 7.5%
d. 0.75%

8. The manager made efforts to <u>temper</u> her criticism with praise so the employee would not feel upset.

In this context, <u>temper</u> most nearly means

a. Anger
b. Combine
c. Soften

9. Look at the row of numbers below.

4 8 24 96 ?

What number should come next?

a. 72
b. 120
c. 384
d. 480

10. A man is packing for a trip. If he packs three shirts, four pairs of pants, and two pairs of socks, how many days can he go without repeating any item of clothing?

a. 2 days
b. 3 days
c. 9 days
d. 24 days

11. Which word does not fit in the following list?

sketch portfolio blueprint painting

12. Three of the four figures below are identical, but rotated. Which one is different?

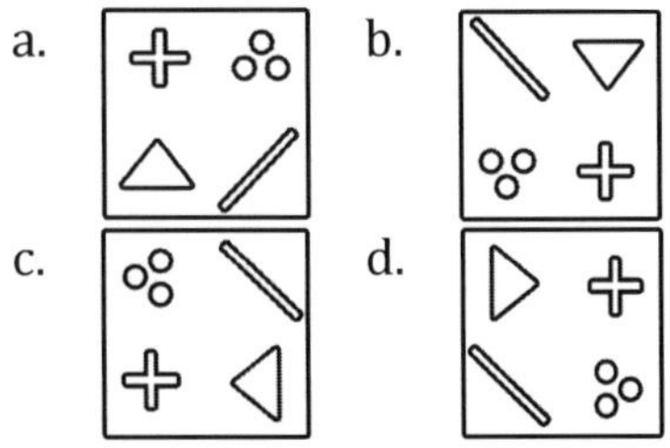

13. Assume the first two statements are true.

1. All soccer team members bring their own ball to practice.
2. Jana is a soccer team member.
3. Jana brings her own ball to practice.

The third statement is:

a. True
b. False
c. Not certain

14. A woman is on vacation for three days and wants to go to a museum, the beach, and the mountains. Assuming she does each activity only once, in how many different orders can she do them?

a. 3
b. 5
c. 6
d. 27

15. If the last day of February is a Sunday, what day will the 28th of March fall on?

a. Sunday
b. Wednesday
c. Friday
d. Saturday

16. How many of the five pairs of items listed below are exact duplicates?

Bob Roberts	Rob Roberts
Shawn Phillips	Shaun Phillips
T.J. Paine	T.J. Paine
Tom Jensen	Tom Jansen
Pete Jacobs	Pete Jacobs

17. A student averaged 80 points on five tests. The first four scores were 78, 74, 82, and 86. What was the score on the last test?

a. 70
b. 75
c. 80
d. 82

18. AUGMENT SUPPLEMENT

These words have:

a. Similar meanings
b. Contradictory meanings
c. Neither similar nor contradictory meanings

19. Look at the row of numbers below. What number should come next?

1 2 0 1 –1 0 ?

a. – 2
b. – 1
c. 0
d. 1

20. It was sunny for ten days in January. January has 31 days. Approximately what percentage of the total days in January was it sunny?

a. 1%
b. 3%
c. 10%
d. 30%

21. Each week, Zach visits his local ice cream shop and orders one of the four flavors randomly. After how many weeks can he ensure having tasted all four flavors?

a. 4
b. 5
c. 8
d. Cannot be determined

22. Which word does not belong with the others?

a. Toaster
b. Oven
c. Appliance
d. Coffee maker

23. Samuel invented more patents than his brother James. Horace had twice as many patents as James. Samuel and Horace had the same number of patents. If the first two statements are true, then the third is:

a. True
b. False
c. Unknown

24. On Frank's bus ride to work, all available seats are filled and 6 passengers are standing in the aisles. If 10 passengers get off the bus and 8 others get on, how many passengers are standing in the aisles, assuming that all available seats continue to be filled?

a. 2
b. 4
c. 6
d. 8

25. The sum of two negative numbers

a. is always negative.
b. is always positive.
c. sometimes is positive and sometimes is negative/
d. is always zero.

26. All of the children are girls. Some of the girls like soccer. Some of the girls like cheerleading. Based on this data, which statement has to be correct?

a. All girls like to play soccer.
b. Some of the girls are 3 years old.
c. Some of the girls like both soccer and cheerleading.
d. Some of the children like soccer.

27. What is the next number in the series?

132, 123, 115, 108, 102

a. 82
b. 87
c. 92
d. 97

28. Otis caught more beads than Steve at Mardi Gras. Steve got as many beads as Carrie. Carrie got fewer beads than Otis. If the first two statements are true, then the third is:

a. True
b. False
c. Unknown

29. Which of the following is the largest number?

a. 1/2
b. 3/8
c. 7/16
d. 13/54

30. Esther drove the same distance as Marcus. Lee drove twice as far as Marcus. Esther drove farther than Lee. If the first two statements are true, then the third is:

a. True
b. False
c. Unknown

Answer Key and Explanations for Test #3

1. B: allow. While "host" is a common meaning of "accommodate," here the gardeners are allowing room for the tree to grow larger in the future.

2. C: 1/3. Each number is found by dividing the previous one by 3. 27 ÷ 3 = 9, and 9 ÷ 3 = 3, and 3 ÷ 3 = 1. 1 ÷ 3 = 1/3, so that is the next number in the series.

3. D: none of these can be logically concluded. We don't know that the reason Miguel doesn't attend school is because he hasn't been vaccinated. He might be an infant, or an adult, for example.

4. A: 2 1/4 cups. To triple the recipe, multiply the numerator (3) by 3, getting 9/4. 4 goes into 9 twice, with 1 left over, so our end result is 2 1/4 cups.

5. A: July. Simply count the months of the year. January, February, March, April, May, June, and July represent seven months.

6. A: This is the only figure in which the three faces shown could appear in that orientation on a cube made from the two-dimensional shape given. In choice B, the two circles could be next to the other two figures, but the three stripes should be facing the other way. In choice C, the two squares should be on the side of the cube we cannot see, if we see the other two figures. In choice D, the arrow and the stripes could not be visible at the same time; they should be on opposite sides of the cube. Choice A is the only one that is logically possible.

7. A: 75%. 0.75 means seventy-five one-hundredths, or 75 parts per hundred. Percent means the same thing: parts per hundred. So 75% is the equivalent to 0.75.

8. C: soften. While "temper" sometimes refers to a person's quickness to anger, here it means to soften. While she is combining the criticism and praise, she is doing so in a specific way that is better described by "soften."

9. D: 480. The series of numbers is formed by multiplying the previous number by increasing factors: 4 × 2 = 8, then 8 × 3 = 24, then 24 × 4 = 96. So the next operation is to multiply 96 by 5, resulting in 480.

10. A: 2 days. This question actually doesn't require any math! To find out how long he can go without repeating any items of clothing, simply look at the category of clothing that has the smallest number of items in it. In this case, it is socks; the man has two pairs of socks. On day three, he'll have to repeat a pair of socks. So the answer is two days with no repeats.

11. B: The other three items in the list are single units, while a portfolio is a collection of items such as these.

12. B: In all three other answer choices, the line stretches across its section of the square, but in choice B, it points into the corner.

13. A: Answer: A, true. If all soccer team members bring their own ball to practice, and Jana is a soccer team member, then she must bring her own ball to practice.

14. C: 6. To find the answer, simply multiply together the woman's available activity choices on each day. On day one, she can do any of the three activities. On day two, she can do either of the remaining two activities, and on day three, she can do the one remaining activity. Multiplying these together, we get 3 × 2 × 1 = 6.

15. A: Sunday. If the last day of February is a Sunday, then the 28th of March falls 28 days later. (This is true whether February has 28 or 29 days in it in a given year.) Because 28 is a multiple of 7, the 28th of March will fall exactly 4 weeks later, on the same day as the last day of February.

16. Two are exact duplicates, T.J. Paine and Pete Jacobs. In the first pair, Bob and Rob do not match. In the second, Shawn and Shaun are spelled differently. In the fourth pair, Jensen and Jansen are spelled differently.

17. C: 80. To find the missing score, work backward. Multiply the average of 80 by the number of tests (in this case, five), then subtract out all the known scores to find the missing score. 80 × 5 = 400, and 400 – 78 –74 – 82 – 86 = 80.

18. A: Answer: A, have similar meanings. Both words refer to increasing the amount of something. "To augment" is to make bigger, while "to supplement" is to add to something.

19. A: –2. There is a two-step pattern going on here. First, we add 1, then we subtract 2. 1 + 1 = 2, then 2 – 2 = 0. 0 + 1 = 1, then 1 – 2 = –1. –1 + 1 = 0, so the next thing to do is subtract 2, giving us –2.

20. D: 30%. Ten out of 31 days is roughly 1/3, or about 30%.

21. D: Just as flipping a coin any number of times could result in the same outcome (heads or tails) each time, ordering randomly (if such a thing is possible) is no guarantee that all flavors will eventually be ordered. This is different from problems in which people select a jelly bean out of a pot and remove it from consideration for the next selection; because jelly beans are removed from consideration, that scenario ensures that all jelly beans will eventually be chosen.

22. C: "Appliance" is a general category that the other words in the list belong to. Toasters, ovens, and coffee makers are all appliances.

23. C: We can diagram the first two sentences as follows: Samuel > James; Horace > James. These sentences do not give us enough information to prove sentence three, Samuel = Horace.

24. B: After the 10 passengers get off the bus, presumably no one will be standing in the aisles and there will be 4 vacant seats. After the 8 new passengers board, 4 of them will fill the vacant seats and the other 4 will be left to stand in the aisles. It is also possible to calculate the answer by assigning any number to the number of seats on the bus. For instance, if there are 20 seats on the bus, then at the start of the problem there are 26 passengers. After 10 get off, there are 16 passengers, and after 8 get on, there are then 24 passengers. The first 20 passengers would fill the available seats, and the other 4 would stand in the aisles.

25. A: Negative numbers represent segments extending to the left of zero on the number line. Adding a negative number to another negative number extends the segment even further to the left, or into "negative territory". To add two negative numbers, add the magnitudes and retain the negative sign. For example

(-3) + (-5) = -8.

26. D: If all of the children are girls, and some of the girls like soccer, then some of the children must like soccer. None of the other statements can be deduced from the information given.

27. D: The pattern is subtracting one less number each time:

132- 9 = 123

123-8 = 115

115-7 = 108

108-6= 102

The next number to be subtracted is 5, so 102-5 = 97

28. A: We can diagram the first two sentences as follows: Otis > Steve = Carrie. The third sentence claims that Otis > Carrie, which is consistent with the first two sentences.

29. A: Convert each to the lowest common denominator and then compare the numerators. Since 2 and 8 are factors of 16, we only need to use 16, 54, and 216 to find the common denominator.

$$16 = 2 \times 2 \times 2 \times 2$$
$$54 = 2 \times 3 \times 3 \times 3$$
$$216 = 2 \times 2 \times 2 \times 3 \times 3 \times 3$$
$$LCD = 2 \times 2 \times 2 \times 2 \times 3 \times 3 \times 3 = 432$$

$$\frac{1}{2} = \frac{216}{432}$$
$$\frac{3}{8} = \frac{162}{432}$$
$$\frac{7}{16} = \frac{189}{432}$$
$$\frac{13}{54} = \frac{104}{432}$$
$$\frac{89}{216} = \frac{178}{432}$$

$216 > 189 > 178 > 162 > 104$. Therefore, 1/2 is the largest fraction.

30. B: The first two sentences can be diagrammed as follows: Esther = Marcus; Lee > Marcus. If Lee drove farther than Marcus, he also drove farther than Esther. The third sentence, which we can diagram as Esther > Lee, contradicts sentences one and two, so it is false.

Wonderlic Skill Building Questions

Mathematics Practice 1

1. 25% of 400 =

a. 100
b. 200
c. 800
d. 10,000

2. 22% of $900 =

a. 90
b. 198
c. 250
d. 325

3. Which of these numbers is a factor of 21?

a. 2
b. 5
c. 7
d. 42

4. (9÷3) x (8÷4) =

a. 1
b. 6
c. 72
d. 576

5. Once inch equals 2.54 cm. How many centimeters tall is a 76- inch man.

a. 20 cm
b. 29.92 cm
c. 193.04 cm
d. 300.04 cm

6. What is the reciprocal of 6?

a. ½
b. 1/3
c. 1/6
d. 1/12

7. A room measures 11 ft x 12 ft x 9 ft. What is the volume?

a. 1188 ft^3
b. 32 ft^3
c. 120 ft^3
d. 1300 ft^3

8. A roast was cooked at 325 °F in the oven for 4 hours. The internal temperature rose from 32 °F to 145 °F. What was the average rise in temperature per hour?

a. 20.2 °F/hr
b. 28.25°F/hr
c. 32.03°F/hr
d. 37°F/hr

9. You need to purchase a textbook for school. The book cost $80.00, and the sales tax where you are purchasing the book is 8.25%. You have $100. How much change will you receive back?

a. $5.20
b. $7.35
c. $13.40
d. $19.95

10. You purchase a car making a down payment of $3,000 and 6 monthly payments of $225. How much have you paid so far for the car?

a. $3225
b. $4350
c. $5375
d. $6550

11. Your supervisor instructs you to purchase 240 pens and 6 staplers for the nurse's station. Pens are purchase in sets of 6 for $2.35 per pack. Staplers are sold in sets of 2 for 12.95. How much will purchasing these products cost?

a. $132.85
b. $145.75
c. $162.90
d. $225.05

12. Which of the following percentages is equal to 0.45?

a. 0.045%
b. 0.45%
c. 4.5%
d. 45%

13. A vitamin's expiration date has passed. It was suppose to contain 500 mg of Calcium, but it has lost 325 mg of Calcium. How many mg of Calcium is left?

a. 135 mg
b. 175 mg
c. 185 mg
d. 200 mg

14. You have orders to give a patient 20 mg of a certain medication. The medication is stored 4 mg per 5-mL dose. How many milliliters will need to be given?

a. 15 mL
b. 20 mL
c. 25 mL
d. 30 mL

15. In the number 743.25 which digit represents the tenths space?

a. 2
b. 3
c. 4
d. 5

16. Which of these percentages equals 1.25?

a. 0.125%
b. 12.5%
c. 125%
d. 1250%

17. If the average person drinks 8, (8oz) glasses of water per day, a person who drinks 12.8 oz of water after a morning exercise session has consumed what fraction of the daily average?

a. 1/3
b. 1/5
c. 1/7
d. 1/9

18. If y = 3, then $y^3(y^3-y)$=

a. 300
b. 459
c. 648
d. 999

19. 33% of 300 =

a. 3
b. 9
c. 33
d. 99

20. You need 4/5 cups of water for a recipe. You accidentally put 1/3 cups into the mixing bowl with the dry ingredients. How much more water in cups do you need to add?

a. 1/3 cups
b. 2/3 cups
c. 1/15 cups
d. 7/15 cups

21. ¾ - ½ =

a. ¼
b. 1/3
c. ½
d. 2/3

22. You cannot find your 1 cup measuring cup. You can only locate your ¼ measuring cup. Your recipe calls for 2 ½ cups of flour. How many times will you need to fill your ¼ measuring cup with flour for the recipe?

a. 4
b. 6
c. 8
d. 10

23. You are financing a computer for $5000. You are required to put down a 15% down payment. How much money do you need for your down payment?

a. $500
b. $650
c. $750
d. $900

24. You are traveling in Europe, and you see a sign stating that London is 3 kilometers away. If 1 kilometer is equal to 0.625 miles, how many miles away is London from where you are?

a. 0.208 miles
b. 1.875 miles
c. 2.75 miles
d. 3 miles

25. You need exactly a 1680 ft3 aquarium for your fish. At the pet store you see four choices of aquariums, but the volume is not listed. The length, width, and height are listed on the box. Which of the following aquariums would fit your needs?

a. 12 ft x 12 ft x 12 ft
b. 13 ft x 15 ft x 16 ft
c. 14 ft x 20 ft x 6 ft
d. 15 ft x 16 ft x 12 ft

26. You invested $9,000 and received yearly interest of $450. What is your interest rate on your investment?

a. 5%
b. 6%
c. 7%
d. 8%

27. In your class there are 48 students, 32 students are female. Approximately what percentage is male?

a. 25%
b. 33%
c. 45%
d. 66%

28. If w = 82 +2, and z = 41 (2), then

a. w<z
b. w>z
c. w-z = 1
d. w=z

29. After talking with his girlfriend on the telephone long distance, a student calculates the amount of money he spent on the call. The first 20 minutes were 99 cents, and each additional minute was 10 cents. He calculated that his phone call cost $ 5.49. How long was his call?

a. 40 minutes
b. 45 minutes
c. 65 minutes
d. 75 minutes

30. You are teaching a community education class on fire safety to children. There are 6 first graders, 7 second graders, and 5 third graders. What percentage of the class are second graders?

a. 28%
b. 33%
c. 39%
d. 48%

31. One slice of bread is 80 calorie. Approximately how many calories are in 2 ½ slices of bread?

a. 140 calories
b. 200 calories
c. 220 calories
d. 240 calories

32. 7x = 3a + 2a. If a = 7, then x =

a. 5
b. 7
c. 9
d. 12

Use the following formula for answering Question 33:

Fried's rule for computing an infant's dose of medication is:

$$\text{infant's dose} = \frac{\text{Child's age in months} \times \text{adult dose}}{150}$$

33. If the adult dose of medication is 15 mg, how much should be given to a 2 year-old child?

a. 1.2
b. 2.4
c. 3.6
d. 4.8

34. What is the area of a triangle if the base is 6 cm and the height is 8 cm.

a. 18 cm^2
b. 20 cm^2
c. 22 cm^2
d. 24 cm^2

35. 7 ½ - 5 3/8 =

a. 1 1/2
b. 1 2/3
c. 2 1/8
d. 3 1/4

36. The school's softball team won 15 games, but lost 10. What was ratio of wins to losses?

a. 2:1
b. 3:1
c. 3:2
d. 4:1

37. 35 is 20% of what number?

a. 175
b. 186
c. 190
d. 220

38. 6 x 0 x 5

a. 30
b. 11
c. 25
d. 0

39. 7.95 ÷ 1.5

a. 2.4
b. 5.3
c. .2
d. 7.3

40. If x = 4, then 2x + 7x =

a. 24
b. 27
c. 35
d. 36

41. 7/10 equals:

a. 0.007
b. 0.07
c. 0.7
d. 1.7

42. 4/8 equals:

a. 0.005
b. 0.05
c. 0.5
d. 5

43. 8/24 equals:

a. 1/6
b. 1/4
c. 1/8
d. 1/3

44. 83,000 equals:

a. 83.0×10^5
b. 8.3×10^4
c. 8.3×10^{-4}
d. 83.0×10^{-3}

45. .00875 equals:

a. 8.75×10^1
b. 8.75×10^{-3}
c. 8.75×10^3
d. 87.5×10^4

46. –32 + 7 equals:

a. –25
b. 25
c. –26
d. 26

47. –37 + -47 equals:

a. 84
b. –84
c. 10
d. –10

48. 41% equals:

a. 4.1
b. 0.41
c. 0.041
d. 0.0041

49. 22(5x) =

a. 110x
b. 4.4 x
c. $110x^2$
d. $4.4\ x^2$

Answer Key for Mathematics Practice 1

1. A: (400 x .25) = 100

2. B: ($900 x .22) = 198

3. C: (Factors are numbers that can divide evenly into a certain number. 7 can divide into 21 three times.)

4. B: (3) x (2) = 6

5. C: 1/2.54 = 76/x; x = 2.54 (76), x= 193.04

6. C: The reciprocal of a fraction is the inverse of the fraction. The fraction is turned upside down. 6 = 6/1, the reciprocal is 1/6.

7. A: 11 ft x 12ft x 19 ft = 1188 ft^3

8. B: 145°F-32°F = 113°F, 113°F ÷4hrs = 28.25°F/ hr

9. C: $80 x 0.825= $6.60, $ 80+ $6.60= $86.60, $100-$86.60= $13.40

10. B: $3000 + ($225(6 payments)= $4350

11. A: 240÷6 = 40, 6÷2=3, (40 packs of pens x $2.35 ea.) + (3 packs of staplers x $12.95 ea.) =$132.85

12. D: .45 x 100 = 45%

13. B: 500mg Ca – 325 mg Ca = 175 mg Ca

14. C: set up ration of 4/5 = 20/x, 4x= 20(5), x = 100/4, x= 25 mL dose

15. A: moving right of the decimal point one space is the tenths position

16. C: 1.25 x 100= 125%

17. B: 12.8 ÷ 64 = .20. .20= 20/100, reduce 20/100 to 1/5

18. C: 27(27-3)= 27(24) = 648

19. D: 300 x .33= 99

20. D: 4/5 –1/3, find common denominator, 12/15-5/15= 7/15 cups

21. A: ¾ - ½ = ¾ - 2/4 = ¼

22. D: 2 ½ converts to 5/2, find common denominator 10/4 ÷ ¼ = 10 cups

23. C: $5000 x .15 = $750

24. B: .625 x 3 = 1.875 miles, you can also set up as a ratio

25. C: 14 ft x 20 ft x 6 ft = 1680 ft^3

26. A: 450 ÷ 9000 = .05, .05 x 100= 5%

27. B: 48 students – 32 girls = 16 boys, 16 ÷ 48= .33, .33 x 100=33%

28. B: w=84, y = 82, 84>82

29. C: .99 + .10 (x) = $5.49, .10 x= 5.49-.99, x= 4.50/.10, x= 45, 45+20=65 mins (Don't forget the original 20 minutes from the flat rate of 99 cents.)

30. C: 7÷18= .39, .39 x 100 = 39%

31. B: 80 calories x 2.5 slices of bread = 200 calories

32. A: 7x= 21+14, 35 ÷ 7 = x, x=5

33. B: infant dose = (24 months ÷ 150) 15 mg= 2.4mg

34. D: ½ (b) (h) = ½ (6) (8)= 24 cm^2

35. C: (15/2) – (43/8)= (60/8)- (43/8)= 17/8 = 2 1/8

36. C: 3:2 both 15 and 10 are divisible by 5

37. A: 20% is 1/5 of a number 1/5 = 35/x. 1x= 35(5), x = 175

38. D: any number multiplied by 0 is equal to 0

39. B: 7.95 ÷1.5= 5.3, remember to move decimal point one place over before beginning equation

40. D: 2(4) + 7(4) = 8 + 28= 36

41. C: 7 Divided by 10 = .7

42. C: 4/8 reduced to ½, 1 divided by 2 = .5

43. D: 8 goes into 8 = 1, 8 goes into 24, = 3

44. B: If the decimal moves to the left the ^{4} is positive.

45. B: If the decimal moves to the right the $^{-3}$ is negative.

46. A: –25, Add the positive and negative numbers together.

47. B: Add the two negative numbers together

48. B: 41 Divided by 100 equals .41

49. A: 110x There are no exponents to multiply together.

Verbal Practice 1

Pick the word that is most appropriate.

1. John prefers ______ art to the classics.

a. Contemporary
b. Contemperary
c. Contemparary
d. Conteporary

2. Allen told Steve that he would give him the ____ version of his morning when he had time.

a. Unabridgged
b. Unabriddged
c. Unabbridged
d. Unabridged

3. Lisa was known for having ______ relationships.

a. Promiscous
b. Promicuous
c. Promiscuous
d. Promicious

4. The new tax was passed for _____ the waterfront district.

a. Revitallizing
b. Revitalizzing
c. Revitelizing
d. Revitalizing

5. The increased ______ to the class fund allowed for an end of the year party.

a. Revenuee
b. Revenue
c. Revanue
d. Revanuee

6. The teenager _____ some candy from the grocery store.

a. Pillferred
b. Pilferred
c. Pillfered
d. Pilfered

7. Being from a small town, some of Dean's views were ______.

a. Parochial
b. Perochial
c. Porochial
d. Parochiel

8. All of the students dreaded the quizzes the professor gave since he tested on ____ material.

a. Obscere
b. Obscore
c. Obbscure
d. Obscure

9. The judge sued the newspaper for ___.

a. Libel
b. Labal
c. Lobel
d. Libbel

Identify the key word/words that complete the statements 10-20.

10. The ____ of the rainbow were ____ against the bright blue sky.

a. Textures, Clear
b. Hues, Vivid
c. Alabaster, Bright
d. Line, Dark

11. The president has a ____ of _____ around him when he makes public appearances.

a. Catalyst, Individuals
b. Barrier, Contrast
c. Hedge, Protection
d. Derrick, Protection

12. A small selection of terms was found at the back of the textbook. It was a

a. Glossary
b. Preface
c. Diction
d. Kefir

13. The horror movie frightened the children. It was

a. Melancholy
b. Dramatic
c. Ghastly
d. Tragedy

14. After practice, the girl's softball team stated, "We're famished!"

Famished means

a. Fatigued
b. Hungry
c. Excited
d. Ready

15. The newborn baby was enamored with the rattle.

Enamored means

a. Fascinated
b. Happy
c. Unsure what to do
d. Aggravated

16. When having a problem, it is best to dissect the situation then act.

Dissect means

a. Cut apart
b. Talk about
c. Ignore
d. Analyze

17. The books subject matter was ____ to the ____, and it did not sell.

a. Attractive, Masses
b. Limited, People
c. Loathsome, Masses
d. Colorful, Individual

18. The kitten was soaked to the ____ from the ___.

a. Skin, Abyss
b. Skin, Craven
c. Skin, Storm
d. Hide, Abyss

19. The bouncer's countenance discouraged brawls.

Countenance means

a. Message
b. Presence
c. Expression
d. Strength

20. The child apprized her father's authority and behaved herself in church.

Apprized means

a. Appreciated
b. Compromised
c. Defied
d. Noted

Identify the appropriate error in the following sentences 21-26.

21. David was known for belching; and telling inappropriate jokes in public.

a. Capitalization
b. Punctuation
c. Spelling
d. Grammar

22. Graduation from High School is considered by many a momentous occasion.

a. Capitalization
b. Punctuation
c. Spelling
d. Grammar

23. Nurses plays a vital role in the healthcare profession.

a. Capitalization
b. Punctuation
c. Spelling
d. Grammar

24. After having his tonsels removed, the child was listless for a few days.

a. Capitalization
b. Punctuation
c. Spelling
d. Grammar

25. The park was serine at twilight.

a. Capitalization
b. Punctuation
c. Spelling
d. Grammar

26. The patient's mind was lucid during the evaluation?

a. Capitalization
b. Punctuation
c. Spelling
d. Grammar

Answer Key for Verbal Practice 1

1. A

2. D

3. C

4. D

5. B

6. D

7. A

8. D

9. A

10. B

11. C

12. A

13. C

14. B

15. A

16. D

17. C

18. C

19. C

20. A

21. B

22. A

23. D

24. C

25. C

26. B

Mathematics Practice 2

1. 75% of 500

a. 365
b. 375
c. 387
d. 390

2. 45% of 600

a. 250
b. 260
c. 270
d. 280

3. (7 x 5) + (8 x 2) =

a. 51
b. 57
c. 85
d. 560

4. (8 ÷ 2) (12 ÷ 3) =

a. 1
b. 8
c. 12
d. 16

5. Which of the following numbers is a prime number?

a. 12
b. 25
c. 27
d. 31

6. Which number is a factor of 36?

a. 5
b. 7
c. 8
d. 9

7. 75 x 34 =

a. 1200
b. 2050
c. 2550
d. 3100

8. x + 372 = 853, x =

a. 455
b. 481
c. 520
d. 635

9. Convert .25 into fraction form.

a. ¼
b. ½
c. 1/8
d. 2/3

10. 60 grains are equal to 1 dram. How many grains are in 15 drams?

a. 900
b. 1020
c. 1220
d. 1300

11. A pitcher holds 7 ½ cups water. How many cups will 5 pitchers hold?

a. 34 ¼
b. 35 ½
c. 37 ½
d. 38 ¼

12. If a = 3, b= 4, c=5, then $(a + b + c)^2 + (a - b - c) =$

a. 124
b. 136
c. 138
d. 150

13. 0.85 =

a. 13/15
b. 17/20
c. 18/19
d. 19/22

14. Which fraction is closest to 2/3 without going over?

a. 6/13
b. 7/12
c. 11/16
d. 9/12

15. A puddle of water contained 72 pints of water. A rainstorm added 21% more water to the puddle. Approximately, how many pints of water are now in the puddle?

a. 76
b. 87
c. 92
d. 112

16. If x = 2 then $x^4 (x + 3) =$

a. 72
b. 80
c. 96
d. 114

17. A circle graph is used to show the percent of patient types that a hospital sees. How many degrees of the circle should the graph show if 1/3 of the patient type is pediatric?

a. 90 degrees
b. 120 degrees
c. 220 degrees
d. 360 degrees

18. A traveler on vacation spent $ 25 at the grocery store the first week of school; the next two weeks he spent $ 52; and the last week he spent $34. What was his average food expenditure while he was on vacation?

a. $ 37.00
b. $ 38.25
c. $ 40.75
d. $ 52.00

19. 437.65 - 325.752 =

a. 111.898
b. 121.758
c. 122.348
d. 133.053

20. 43.3 x 23.03 =

a. 997.199
b. 999.999
c. 1010.03
d. 1111.01

21. How many nonoverlapping 2-inch x 2-inch squares are contained in a 8-inch x 24- inch rectangle?

a. 32
b. 44
c. 48
d. 52

22. After going on diet for two weeks, you have lost 6% of you weight. Your original weight was 157 lbs. What do you weigh now?

a. 132 lbs
b. 135.48 lbs
c. 144.98 lbs
d. 147.58 lbs

23. In order for a school to allow a vending machine to be placed next to the cafeteria, 65% of the school's population must ask for it. If 340 of the school's 650 students have requested the vending machines, how many more are needed to get the vending machines?

a. 75
b. 83
c. 89
d. 99

24. After purchasing a book that has a no return policy, the book goes on sale at the bookstore for 15% less. You realize that you spent an extra $12.75 on the book. What amount did you pay for the book originally?

a. $65
b. $75
c. $85
d. $95

25. Which of the following fractions have the largest value?

a. 8/15
b. 7/12
c. 6/13
d. 9/16

26. Round this number to the nearest hundredths 390.24657

a. 400
b. 390.247
c. 390.25
d. 390.2

27. To get 1 as an answer, you must multiply 4/5 by

a. 5/4
b. ½
c. 1
d. ¼

28. z = 4, z + 6 – (z+4)=

a. 2
b. 4
c. 6
d. 8

29. While working, patient's sodium intake was 300 mg on Monday, 1240 mg on Tuesday, 900 mg on Wednesday and Friday, and 1500 on Thursday. What was the average intake of sodium while the patient was at work?

a. 476 mg
b. 754 mg
c. 968 mg
d. 998 mg

30. Which of the following numbers is correctly rounded to the nearest tenth?

a. 3.756 rounds to 3.76
b. 4.567 rounds to 4.5
c. 6.982 rounds to 7.0
d. 54.32 rounds to 54.4

31. 4.2% of 328 =

a. 12.7
b. 13.8
c. 14.2
d. 15.5

32. Which of the following fraction equal 0.625

a. 3/4
b. 5/6
c. 5/8
d. 2/3

33. Which of the following illustrates the distributive property of multiplication?

a. $2x + 5(z - 3) = 10x + 5z - 15$
b. $2x + 5(z - 3) = 2x + 5z - 3$
c. $2x + 5(z - 3) = 2x + 5z - 15$
d. $2x + 5(z - 3) = 2z + z - 15$

34. Which of the following is the square root of 80

a. $4\sqrt{5}$
b. 8
c. $5\sqrt{4}$
d. 16

Questions 35 to 38 refer to the following information:

A school has a 50 x 60 yard rectangular playground. There are 3 classes playing on it. 15 students are from Mrs. Red's class, 12 are from Miss White's class, and 17 are from Ms. Brown's class.

35. How many square yards does the playground cover?

a. 110
b. 300
c. 3,000
d. 30,000

36. How many students are playing on the playground?

a. 15
b. 22
c. 36
d. 44

37. If both sides of the playground are increased by 10%, what would the area be in square yards?

a. 121
b. 1210
c. 3,000
d. 3,630

38. Ms. Brown's class raised $400 to help put a fence around the playground. The fence cost $15 a yard. How much more money per student would Ms. Brown's class have to raise to completely fence in the playground?

a. $165.12
b. $170.59
c. $183.57
d. $220.25

39. 160%=

a. 5/6
b. 6/5
c. 8/5
d. 9/6

40. A 6% (by volume) solution of bleach in water is required for cleaning a bathroom. How many milliliters of the solution can be made from 50 milliliters of pure bleach?

a. 833
b. 952
c. 1054
d. 2000

41. 8.7 x 23.3 equals:

a. 202.71
b. 2027.1
c. 212.71
d. 2127.1

42. 134.5 Divided by 5 equals:

a. 26.9
b. 25.9
c. 23.9
d. 22.9

43. 5.30 x 10^{-4} equals:

a. 0.000053
b. 0.00053
c. 53,000
d. 5,300,000

44. 23/3 =

a. 6 2/3
b. 7 1/3
c. 7 2/3
d. 8 1/3

45. 33/100 =

a. 0.0033
b. 0.033
c. 0.33
d. 3.3

46. $45^x/5^x$ =

a. 9^x
b. 9
c. 11^x
d. 11

47. 24x/3 =

a. 8x
b. 8
c. 7x
d. 7

48. 52x(4y) =

a. 13xy
b. 13xy
c. $208x^{-y}$
d. 208xy

49. 4500 + 3422 + 3909 =

a. 12,831
b. 12,731
c. 11,831
d. 11,731

Answer Key for Mathematics Practice 2

1. B: (500 x .75) = 375

2. C: (600 x .45) = 270

3. A: (35 +16 =51)

4. D: (4 x 4 = 16)

5. D: (31 is a prime number; it is only divisible by itself and one)

6. D: (A factor is a number that divides evenly into another number.)

7. C: (75 x 34 = 2550)

8. B: (853-372= 481)

9. A

10. A: (60 x 15 = 900)

11. C: (15/2) (10/2) = 150/4 = 37.5

12. C: (144) + (-6)= 138

13. B: (85/100) reduces to 17/20

14. B: Divide all fractions into decimals and compare

15. B: (72 x .21= 15.12) 15.12+ 72= 87.12≈ 87pints

16. B: (2 x 2 x 2 x 2) (5) = 16 x 5 = 80

17. B: (360 degrees ÷ 3 = 120 degrees)

18. C: ($25 + $52 + $52 + $34= $163) $163 ÷ 4 = $40.75

19. A: (437.65-325.752 = 111.898)

20. A: (43.3 x 23.03 = 997.199)

21. C: (2 x 2= 4) , (8 x 24 = 192) 192 in^2 ÷ 4 in^2 = 48

22. D: (157 lbs x .06 = 9.42 lbs) 157lbs- 9.42 lbs =147.58lbs

23. B: (650 students x .65 = 422.5) 422.5 – 340 = 82.5 ≈ 83 more students

24. C: (15/100 = 12.75/x) 15x= (100) (12.75) x= 1275/15 = $85

25. B: (Divide out all fractions and compare decimal equivalents)

26. C: (the hundredths place is two right of the decimal point)

27. A: (to get one multiple any fraction by its reciprocal)

28. A: (4 + 6 – (4 + 4) = 2 (work inside of the parentheses first

29. C: (300mg + 120 mg + 900mg + 900mg + 1500mg = 4840mg, 4840mg ÷ 5 = 968 mg

30. C: (6.982 rounds to 7.0) look at the 8 it rounds the 9 to a 10 which adds a one to the ones place, the 0 holds the tenths place

31. B: (.042 x 328 = 13.8)

32. C: (change into fraction form 625/1000 then reduce)

33. C: (multiply everything within the parentheses only)

34. A: Break 80 down into (16) (5), 16 has a square root of 4 leaving 5

35. C: (50 x 60 = 3000)

36. D: (15 + 12 + 17= 44)

37. D: (50 x .1 = 5), 50+5=55, (60 x .1 = 6), 60 + 6 = 66, 66 x 55 = 3630 square yards

38. B: (60 + 60 + 50 + 50 = 220), (220 yards x $15/ yard = $3,300) (3,300 – 400= 2,900), (2,900 ÷17 = $170.59)

39. C: (8/5 = 1.6) 1.6 x 100 = 160%

40. A: (set up a ratio of 6/100 = 50/x) then solve by cross multiplying

41. A: Straight multiplication

42. A: Straight division

43. B: In scientific notation, the exponent on the 10 is the key to determining the decimal equivalent. A negative exponent means the value is decimal less than 1 in other words, move the decimal point to the left. In this case, it will move 4 places:

$$\begin{aligned} 5.30 \times 10^{-4} &= 5.3 \times 0.0001 \\ &= 0.00053 \end{aligned}$$

44. C: 7 2/3

45. C: 33 Divided by 100 = 0.33

46. A: Begin by factoring 45^x into 9^x and 5^x, since $45^x = (9 \times 5)^x = 9^x \times 5^x$. The 5^x cancels out and the remainder is 9^x.

47. A: Exponents do not cancel out.

48. D: Straight multiplication of numbers and exponents

49. C: Straight addition

Verbal Practice 2

Pick the word that is most appropriate.

1. Susan's _____ of darkness prevents her from leaving her house at night. means

a. Abhorance
b. Abhorence
c. Abhorrence
d. Abhorrance

2. The girl displayed ____ behavior when she found out her puppy was injured.

a. Destraught
b. Distaught
c. Distraught
d. Distrauht

3. The French exchange student spoke English as if it were her first language. She was

a. Dandy
b. Fluent
c. Caustic
d. Talented

4. The prescription plan did not cover name brand drugs if there was a ______ substitute available.

a. Generic
b. Reasonable
c. Compatible
d. Complete

5. The ______ crowd mourned the loss of their leader.

a. Sember
b. Somber
c. Sombar
d. Sombor

6. The southern ____ girl was known for her behavior.

a. Gentell
b. Ganteel
c. Genteal
d. Genteel

7. The mother attempted to _____ her son with toys.

a. Molifey
b. Mollify
c. Molify
d. Mollifey

8. The car accident caused a sliver of glass to cut the passenger's optic nerve. The passenger lost his

a. Arm
b. Movement
c. Smell
d. Vision

9. Some people accused John of thinking too much. He would sometimes ___ on a subject for months at a time.

a. Pondar
b. Pondder
c. Ponnder
d. Ponder

10. The young artist had an ______ passion for watercolors.

a. Unbradled
b. Unbriddled
c. Unbridled
d. Unbridlled

11. The _____ kept the students cool while they sat outside studying.

a. Zephyir
b. Zepheyer
c. Zepyr
d. Zephyr

12. The pianist played his rendition of a _____.

a. Sonata
b. Sonatina
c. Sonate
d. Sonete

13. The entertainer had no _____ about performing in front of two thousand screaming fans.

a. Qulams
b. Quelms
c. Qualms
d. Qualmes

14. The _____ still enjoyed being around its mother but was acting more independent each day.

a. Yearling
b. Yeerling
c. Yearlling
d. Yearlinng

15. The financial planner had reached the top of his career; he felt he was at his

a. Performance
b. Stress level
c. Limit
d. Zenith

16. The siblings found ____ in each other as they ___ the good times with their father.

a. Happiness, Prepared
b. Sorrow, Committed
c. Solace, Remembered
d. Sorrow, Limited

17. The young boy sat _____ as the principal yelled at him.

a. Passivly
b. Pasively
c. Passivelly
d. Passively

18. The teenage was accused of killing his father and mother. He was accused of

a. Sobriety
b. Misguidance
c. Misgamy
d. Parricide

19. Brian's secret to studying success relied on a system designed to assist with the recollection of terms. His secret was the use of

a. Syllables
b. Memorabilia
c. Mnemonics
d. Puzzles

Identify the appropriate error in the following sentences.

20. The bachalor never married. Most people thought it was because of misogyny.

a. Capitalization
b. Punctuation
c. Spelling
d. Grammar

21. The intricacy of the mathematical equation, drove the student crazy trying to solve it.

a. Capitalization
b. Punctuation
c. Spelling
d. Grammar

22. The hybrid tomatoes is immune to most common diseases.

a. Capitalization
b. Punctuation
c. Spelling
d. Grammar

23. The professor was humiliated when his students reported him to the Dean for verbal abuse.

a. Capitalization
b. Punctuation
c. Spelling
d. Grammar

24. The con artist hoodwinked the old lady when he sold her fradulent insurance.

a. Capitalization
b. Punctuation
c. Spelling
d. Grammar

25. The movie star was accused of a misdemeanor, when she stole 15 dollars worth of merchandise from the store.

a. Capitalization
b. Punctuation
c. Spelling
d. Grammar

26. The congregation sang a comtemporary hymn.

a. Capitalization
b. Punctuation
c. Spelling
d. Grammar

Answer Key for Verbal Practice 2

1. C
2. C
3. B
4. A
5. B
6. D
7. B
8. D
9. D
10. C
11. D
12. A
13. C
14. A
15. D
16. C
17. D
18. D
19. C
20. C
21. B
22. D
23. A
24. C
25. B
26. C

How to Overcome Test Anxiety

Just the thought of taking a test is enough to make most people a little nervous. A test is an important event that can have a long-term impact on your future, so it's important to take it seriously and it's natural to feel anxious about performing well. But just because anxiety is normal, that doesn't mean that it's helpful in test taking, or that you should simply accept it as part of your life. Anxiety can have a variety of effects. These effects can be mild, like making you feel slightly nervous, or severe, like blocking your ability to focus or remember even a simple detail.

If you experience test anxiety—whether severe or mild—it's important to know how to beat it. To discover this, first you need to understand what causes test anxiety.

Causes of Test Anxiety

While we often think of anxiety as an uncontrollable emotional state, it can actually be caused by simple, practical things. One of the most common causes of test anxiety is that a person does not feel adequately prepared for their test. This feeling can be the result of many different issues such as poor study habits or lack of organization, but the most common culprit is time management. Starting to study too late, failing to organize your study time to cover all of the material, or being distracted while you study will mean that you're not well prepared for the test. This may lead to cramming the night before, which will cause you to be physically and mentally exhausted for the test. Poor time management also contributes to feelings of stress, fear, and hopelessness as you realize you are not well prepared but don't know what to do about it.

Other times, test anxiety is not related to your preparation for the test but comes from unresolved fear. This may be a past failure on a test, or poor performance on tests in general. It may come from comparing yourself to others who seem to be performing better or from the stress of living up to expectations. Anxiety may be driven by fears of the future—how failure on this test would affect your educational and career goals. These fears are often completely irrational, but they can still negatively impact your test performance.

Elements of Test Anxiety

As mentioned earlier, test anxiety is considered to be an emotional state, but it has physical and mental components as well. Sometimes you may not even realize that you are suffering from test anxiety until you notice the physical symptoms. These can include trembling hands, rapid heartbeat, sweating, nausea, and tense muscles. Extreme anxiety may lead to fainting or vomiting. Obviously, any of these symptoms can have a negative impact on testing. It is important to recognize them as soon as they begin to occur so that you can address the problem before it damages your performance.

The mental components of test anxiety include trouble focusing and inability to remember learned information. During a test, your mind is on high alert, which can help you recall information and stay focused for an extended period of time. However, anxiety interferes with your mind's natural processes, causing you to blank out, even on the questions you know well. The strain of testing during anxiety makes it difficult to stay focused, especially on a test that may take several hours. Extreme anxiety can take a huge mental toll, making it difficult not only to recall test information but even to understand the test questions or pull your thoughts together.

Effects of Test Anxiety

Test anxiety is like a disease—if left untreated, it will get progressively worse. Anxiety leads to poor performance, and this reinforces the feelings of fear and failure, which in turn lead to poor performances on subsequent tests. It can grow from a mild nervousness to a crippling condition. If allowed to progress, test anxiety can have a big impact on your schooling, and consequently on your future.

Test anxiety can spread to other parts of your life. Anxiety on tests can become anxiety in any stressful situation, and blanking on a test can turn into panicking in a job situation. But fortunately, you don't have to let anxiety rule your testing and determine your grades. There are a number of relatively simple steps you can take to move past anxiety and function normally on a test and in the rest of life.

Physical Steps for Beating Test Anxiety

While test anxiety is a serious problem, the good news is that it can be overcome. It doesn't have to control your ability to think and remember information. While it may take time, you can begin taking steps today to beat anxiety.

Just as your first hint that you may be struggling with anxiety comes from the physical symptoms, the first step to treating it is also physical. Rest is crucial for having a clear, strong mind. If you are tired, it is much easier to give in to anxiety. But if you establish good sleep habits, your body and mind will be ready to perform optimally, without the strain of exhaustion. Additionally, sleeping well helps you to retain information better, so you're more likely to recall the answers when you see the test questions.

Getting good sleep means more than going to bed on time. It's important to allow your brain time to relax. Take study breaks from time to time so it doesn't get overworked, and don't study right before bed. Take time to rest your mind before trying to rest your body, or you may find it difficult to fall asleep.

Along with sleep, other aspects of physical health are important in preparing for a test. Good nutrition is vital for good brain function. Sugary foods and drinks may give a burst of energy but this burst is followed by a crash, both physically and emotionally. Instead, fuel your body with protein and vitamin-rich foods.

Also, drink plenty of water. Dehydration can lead to headaches and exhaustion, especially if your brain is already under stress from the rigors of the test. Particularly if your test is a long one, drink water during the breaks. And if possible, take an energy-boosting snack to eat between sections.

Along with sleep and diet, a third important part of physical health is exercise. Maintaining a steady workout schedule is helpful, but even taking 5-minute study breaks to walk can help get your blood pumping faster and clear your head. Exercise also releases endorphins, which contribute to a positive feeling and can help combat test anxiety.

When you nurture your physical health, you are also contributing to your mental health. If your body is healthy, your mind is much more likely to be healthy as well. So take time to rest, nourish your body with healthy food and water, and get moving as much as possible. Taking these physical steps will make you stronger and more able to take the mental steps necessary to overcome test anxiety.

Mental Steps for Beating Test Anxiety

Working on the mental side of test anxiety can be more challenging, but as with the physical side, there are clear steps you can take to overcome it. As mentioned earlier, test anxiety often stems from lack of preparation, so the obvious solution is to prepare for the test. Effective studying may be the most important weapon you have for beating test anxiety, but you can and should employ several other mental tools to combat fear.

First, boost your confidence by reminding yourself of past success—tests or projects that you aced. If you're putting as much effort into preparing for this test as you did for those, there's no reason you should expect to fail here. Work hard to prepare; then trust your preparation.

Second, surround yourself with encouraging people. It can be helpful to find a study group, but be sure that the people you're around will encourage a positive attitude. If you spend time with others who are anxious or cynical, this will only contribute to your own anxiety. Look for others who are motivated to study hard from a desire to succeed, not from a fear of failure.

Third, reward yourself. A test is physically and mentally tiring, even without anxiety, and it can be helpful to have something to look forward to. Plan an activity following the test, regardless of the outcome, such as going to a movie or getting ice cream.

When you are taking the test, if you find yourself beginning to feel anxious, remind yourself that you know the material. Visualize successfully completing the test. Then take a few deep, relaxing breaths and return to it. Work through the questions carefully but with confidence, knowing that you are capable of succeeding.

Developing a healthy mental approach to test taking will also aid in other areas of life. Test anxiety affects more than just the actual test—it can be damaging to your mental health and even contribute to depression. It's important to beat test anxiety before it becomes a problem for more than testing.

Study Strategy

Being prepared for the test is necessary to combat anxiety, but what does being prepared look like? You may study for hours on end and still not feel prepared. What you need is a strategy for test prep. The next few pages outline our recommended steps to help you plan out and conquer the challenge of preparation.

Step 1: Scope Out the Test

Learn everything you can about the format (multiple choice, essay, etc.) and what will be on the test. Gather any study materials, course outlines, or sample exams that may be available. Not only will this help you to prepare, but knowing what to expect can help to alleviate test anxiety.

Step 2: Map Out the Material

Look through the textbook or study guide and make note of how many chapters or sections it has. Then divide these over the time you have. For example, if a book has 15 chapters and you have five days to study, you need to cover three chapters each day. Even better, if you have the time, leave an extra day at the end for overall review after you have gone through the material in depth.

If time is limited, you may need to prioritize the material. Look through it and make note of which sections you think you already have a good grasp on, and which need review. While you are studying, skim quickly through the familiar sections and take more time on the challenging parts.

Write out your plan so you don't get lost as you go. Having a written plan also helps you feel more in control of the study, so anxiety is less likely to arise from feeling overwhelmed at the amount to cover.

Step 3: Gather Your Tools

Decide what study method works best for you. Do you prefer to highlight in the book as you study and then go back over the highlighted portions? Or do you type out notes of the important information? Or is it helpful to make flashcards that you can carry with you? Assemble the pens, index cards, highlighters, post-it notes, and any other materials you may need so you won't be distracted by getting up to find things while you study.

If you're having a hard time retaining the information or organizing your notes, experiment with different methods. For example, try color-coding by subject with colored pens, highlighters, or post-it notes. If you learn better by hearing, try recording yourself reading your notes so you can listen while in the car, working out, or simply sitting at your desk. Ask a friend to quiz you from your flashcards, or try teaching someone the material to solidify it in your mind.

Step 4: Create Your Environment

It's important to avoid distractions while you study. This includes both the obvious distractions like visitors and the subtle distractions like an uncomfortable chair (or a too-comfortable couch that makes you want to fall asleep). Set up the best study environment possible: good lighting and a comfortable work area. If background music helps you focus, you may want to turn it on, but otherwise keep the room quiet. If you are using a computer to take notes, be sure you don't have any other windows open, especially applications like social media, games, or anything else that could distract you. Silence your phone and turn off notifications. Be sure to keep water close by so you stay hydrated while you study (but avoid unhealthy drinks and snacks).

Also, take into account the best time of day to study. Are you freshest first thing in the morning? Try to set aside some time then to work through the material. Is your mind clearer in the afternoon or evening? Schedule your study session then. Another method is to study at the same time of day that you will take the test, so that your brain gets used to working on the material at that time and will be ready to focus at test time.

Step 5: Study!

Once you have done all the study preparation, it's time to settle into the actual studying. Sit down, take a few moments to settle your mind so you can focus, and begin to follow your study plan. Don't give in to distractions or let yourself procrastinate. This is your time to prepare so you'll be ready to fearlessly approach the test. Make the most of the time and stay focused.

Of course, you don't want to burn out. If you study too long you may find that you're not retaining the information very well. Take regular study breaks. For example, taking five minutes out of every hour to walk briskly, breathing deeply and swinging your arms, can help your mind stay fresh.

As you get to the end of each chapter or section, it's a good idea to do a quick review. Remind yourself of what you learned and work on any difficult parts. When you feel that you've mastered the material, move on to the next part. At the end of your study session, briefly skim through your notes again.

But while review is helpful, cramming last minute is NOT. If at all possible, work ahead so that you won't need to fit all your study into the last day. Cramming overloads your brain with more information than it can process and retain, and your tired mind may struggle to recall even previously learned information when it is overwhelmed with last-minute study. Also, the urgent nature of cramming and the stress placed on your brain contribute to anxiety. You'll be more likely to go to the test feeling unprepared and having trouble thinking clearly.

So don't cram, and don't stay up late before the test, even just to review your notes at a leisurely pace. Your brain needs rest more than it needs to go over the information again. In fact, plan to finish your studies by noon or early afternoon the day before the test. Give your brain the rest of the day to relax or focus on other things, and get a good night's sleep. Then you will be fresh for the test and better able to recall what you've studied.

Step 6: Take a Practice Test

Many courses offer sample tests, either online or in the study materials. This is an excellent resource to check whether you have mastered the material, as well as to prepare for the test format and environment.

Check the test format ahead of time: the number of questions, the type (multiple choice, free response, etc.), and the time limit. Then create a plan for working through them. For example, if you have 30 minutes to take a 60-question test, your limit is 30 seconds per question. Spend less time on the questions you know well so that you can take more time on the difficult ones.

If you have time to take several practice tests, take the first one open book, with no time limit. Work through the questions at your own pace and make sure you fully understand them. Gradually work up to taking a test under test conditions: sit at a desk with all study materials put away and set a timer. Pace yourself to make sure you finish the test with time to spare and go back to check your answers if you have time.

After each test, check your answers. On the questions you missed, be sure you understand why you missed them. Did you misread the question (tests can use tricky wording)? Did you forget the information? Or was it something you hadn't learned? Go back and study any shaky areas that the practice tests reveal.

Taking these tests not only helps with your grade, but also aids in combating test anxiety. If you're already used to the test conditions, you're less likely to worry about it, and working through tests until you're scoring well gives you a confidence boost. Go through the practice tests until you feel comfortable, and then you can go into the test knowing that you're ready for it.

Test Tips

On test day, you should be confident, knowing that you've prepared well and are ready to answer the questions. But aside from preparation, there are several test day strategies you can employ to maximize your performance.

First, as stated before, get a good night's sleep the night before the test (and for several nights before that, if possible). Go into the test with a fresh, alert mind rather than staying up late to study.

Try not to change too much about your normal routine on the day of the test. It's important to eat a nutritious breakfast, but if you normally don't eat breakfast at all, consider eating just a protein bar. If you're a coffee drinker, go ahead and have your normal coffee. Just make sure you time it so that the caffeine doesn't wear off right in the middle of your test. Avoid sugary beverages, and drink enough water to stay hydrated but not so much that you need a restroom break 10 minutes into the test. If your test isn't first thing in the morning, consider going for a walk or doing a light workout before the test to get your blood flowing.

Allow yourself enough time to get ready, and leave for the test with plenty of time to spare so you won't have the anxiety of scrambling to arrive in time. Another reason to be early is to select a good seat. It's helpful to sit away from doors and windows, which can be distracting. Find a good seat, get out your supplies, and settle your mind before the test begins.

When the test begins, start by going over the instructions carefully, even if you already know what to expect. Make sure you avoid any careless mistakes by following the directions.

Then begin working through the questions, pacing yourself as you've practiced. If you're not sure on an answer, don't spend too much time on it, and don't let it shake your confidence. Either skip it and come back later, or eliminate as many wrong answers as possible and guess among the remaining ones. Don't dwell on these questions as you continue—put them out of your mind and focus on what lies ahead.

Be sure to read all of the answer choices, even if you're sure the first one is the right answer. Sometimes you'll find a better one if you keep reading. But don't second-guess yourself if you do immediately know the answer. Your gut instinct is usually right. Don't let test anxiety rob you of the information you know.

If you have time at the end of the test (and if the test format allows), go back and review your answers. Be cautious about changing any, since your first instinct tends to be correct, but make sure you didn't misread any of the questions or accidentally mark the wrong answer choice. Look over any you skipped and make an educated guess.

At the end, leave the test feeling confident. You've done your best, so don't waste time worrying about your performance or wishing you could change anything. Instead, celebrate the successful completion of this test. And finally, use this test to learn how to deal with anxiety even better next time.

Review Video: Test Anxiety
Visit mometrix.com/academy and enter code: 100340

Important Qualification

Not all anxiety is created equal. If your test anxiety is causing major issues in your life beyond the classroom or testing center, or if you are experiencing troubling physical symptoms related to your anxiety, it may be a sign of a serious physiological or psychological condition. If this sounds like your situation, we strongly encourage you to seek professional help.

Online Resources

Due to our efforts to try to keep this book to a manageable length, we've created a link that will give you access to all of your online resources:

mometrix.com/resources719/wonderlicwptq

It's Your Moment, Let's Celebrate It!

Share your story @mometrixtestpreparation